THE BRIDEGROOM MESSIAH
The Cross: Love's Greatest Story

Colin Hamer

WIPF & STOCK · Eugene, Oregon

Wipf and Stock Publishers
199 W 8th Ave, Suite 3
Eugene, OR 97401

The Bridegroom Messiah
The Cross:Love's Greatest Story
By Hamer, Colin
Copyright©2018 Apostolos
ISBN 13: 978-1-5326-6916-3
Publication date 9/23/2018
Previously published by Apostolos, 2018

For Lois

CONTENTS

PREFACE 7
GOD THE HUSBAND OF ISRAEL 8
JESUS THE BRIDEGROOM MESSIAH 23
THE NEW COVENANT 37
THE CROSS 53
SOME REFLECTIONS 64

PREFACE

This book looks to tell the Bible's story of mankind's exile from God's presence in the Garden of Eden, to the great climax of history, when Jesus, the Bridegroom Messiah, will come for the church, his bride, and take her to himself so that she might live for ever with him in a new heavens and new earth.

It will tell the story the way the Bible tells it—as a love story between God and his people expressed in marital language that involves separation and divorce, the blood of Jesus shed on the cross to cleanse his bride, and a glorious new marriage at the end of time.

Colin Hamer

January 2018

CHAPTER ONE

GOD THE HUSBAND OF ISRAEL

GOD'S RELATIONSHIP WITH ISRAEL

A Marriage at Mount Sinai

I want to start the story, not at the beginning, but at Mount Sinai. Here God made a covenant with Israel, gave them the Ten Commandments, and took them as his people. The nation understood this relationship as a "marriage," and that the covenant God had given them was their wedding ring. It demonstrated to the rest of the world that they were God's special people.

Although many believe that it is Hosea who introduced and developed this marital theme, the language of the Pentateuch (the first five books of the Bible) only makes sense in light of that concept. Thus Exodus 34:15–16; Leviticus 17:7, 20:5–6; Numbers 25:1–3; and Deuteronomy 31:16 all speak about Israel "whoring" after other gods—in other words they were not being faithful to their "husband." Deuteronomy 33:3 says that God "loved his people," and in ancient Semitic societies marriage is often signified when the verb "to take" is used, and that same verb is used in Exodus 6:7 ("I will take you to be my people") to express God's choice of Israel.

Furthermore, at the Sinai event itself, the account of the golden calf being ground to powder and the people being forced to drink it (Exodus 32:20) appears to be a reference to the Numbers 5:12–31 ordeal for the suspected adulteress. It seems that Israel had been unfaithful on her wedding night! When God eventually promises a new covenant he specifically says, "I was [Israel's] husband" (Jeremiah 31:32).

Marital Imagery

This is called "marital imagery"—where we are asked to *imagine* that God is married to Israel. It is based on a metaphor, and every metaphor has as its basis a statement that "A" is "B," when the statement itself is not literally true. The metaphor in the Bible's marital imagery is that GOD IS THE HUSBAND OF HIS PEOPLE.

It is only in the last 70 years or so that linguists have investigated metaphors and realised that there is often more to them than a poetic flourish. An example of the latter is in Song of Solomon 2:1 where the speaker says, "I am a rose of Sharon, a lily of the valleys." This is what might be called a rhetorical statement used for effect. The only thing we learn is perhaps something about how the speaker feels about himself. However, the Old Testament marital imagery metaphor (that GOD IS THE HUSBAND OF HIS PEOPLE) is not a "rhetorical" metaphor used for effect, but rather a "conceptual" metaphor, that gives us a new understanding about God by describing one thing (his relationship with his people), in terms of another (human marriage). We will see that the Bible's marital imagery gives a deeper insight into the identity of Jesus and why he came.

A Difficult Marriage

After the bad start at Sinai, Israel's subsequent relationship with God continued to be turbulent. Israel consistently disobeyed God and turned their back on him to worship other gods. Judges 21:25 says of the period before the kings ruled that, "Everyone did what was right in his own eyes." Kings and Chronicles continue the sorry story of apostasy, and the split of the nation between the north (Israel) and the south (Judah). All the kings of Israel, and some in Judah, were ungodly. Thus 2 Kings 8:18 says of Jehoram, king of Judah, "And he walked in the way of the kings of Israel, as the house of Ahab had done … he did what was evil in the sight of the LORD."

And so the prophet Hosea was told, "Go, take to yourself a wife of whoredom and have children of whoredom, for the land commits great whoredom by forsaking the LORD" (Hosea 1:2)—it seems that God was saying to Hosea: "I will show you, and thus all Israel, what it is to have a wife like Israel!" But nothing changed, and thus we read in 2 Kings:

> The king of Assyria captured Samaria, and he carried the Israelites away to Assyria … this occurred because the people of Israel had sinned against the LORD their God … they did

> wicked things, provoking the LORD to anger, and they served idols, of which the LORD had said to them, "You shall not do this." Yet the LORD warned Israel and Judah by every prophet and every seer, saying, "Turn from your evil ways and keep my commandments and my statutes, in accordance with all the Law that I commanded your fathers, and that I sent to you by my servants the prophets." But they would not listen ... They despised his statutes and his covenant that he made with their fathers and the warnings that he gave them. They went after false idols. (2 Kings 17:6–15)

Then in v. 18 we read, "Therefore the LORD was very angry with Israel and removed them out of his sight. None was left but the tribe of Judah only."

This break in God's relationship with the northern kingdom occurred in 722 BCE and is known as the Assyrian exile. In Jeremiah 3:1–8 (and elsewhere in the Old Testament) it is described as a "divorce." But many Christians are not happy about understanding the Bible's marital imagery this way, and think that when the Old Testament prophets talk of God "divorcing" Israel, they are using the metaphor simply to make the point that Israel had displeased him. In other words, the prophets did not mean to imply that God would sever his relationship with Israel. This understanding, at least in part, seems to be because many of the Reformers of the 16th century taught that, in contrast to the conditional, temporary covenant Adam had with God based on Adam's obedience, the Mosaic and new covenants were both permanent "covenants of grace" built on a promise given to Abraham. And thus the Mosaic and new covenants could be considered, as John Calvin expressed it in his Christian Institutes (2.10.2), as "one and the same." William Dumbrell, in *Covenant and Creation* (2013), reflects that view, saying that, "the covenant with Israel could not be sundered." However, Jeremiah says that the new covenant is "not like" the Mosaic covenant, and that both Israel and Judah "broke" that covenant:

> Behold, the days are coming, declares the Lord, when I will make a new covenant with the house of Israel and the house of Judah, not like the covenant that I made with their fathers

> on the day when I took them by the hand to bring them out of the land of Egypt, my covenant that they broke, though I was their husband, declares the Lord. (Jeremiah 31:31–32)

Dumbrell himself goes on to point out that the Sinai covenant was tied to political forms and a territorial state and that the stability of this depended upon Israel's response.[i]

Certainly, the Old Testament repeatedly and specifically says that Israel's relationship with God, and their place in the promised land was, like the covenant with Adam, conditional on them keeping within the covenant conditions—for example, Exodus 19:5; Leviticus 18:26–28; Deuteronomy 4:25–26; and Isaiah 48:18–19. They are conditions that Israel manifestly failed to keep, and the consequences of this are spelt out in stark terms:

> I will cut off Israel from the land that I have given them, and the house that I have consecrated for my name I will cast out of my sight, and Israel will become a proverb and a byword among all peoples. And this house will become a heap of ruins. Everyone passing by it will be astonished and will hiss, and they will say, "Why has the LORD done thus to this land and to this house?" (1 Kings 9:7–8)

These verses make it clear that the land and the temple were integral to God's covenant with Israel, and history shows that they lost both. Israel lost most of the land in the Assyrian exile, leaving Judah with just a small area in the south (which, however, included the temple at Jerusalem). But these were also eventually lost, this time in the destruction of Jerusalem in 70 CE. And as both the Assyrian exile, and the destruction of Jerusalem, were at God's specific decree (Isaiah 10:5; Matthew 23:27–38) it is clear that the covenant had been terminated by God. Thus the marital imagery, and the "divorce" it speaks of, is not a rhetorical device. God is using it to teach an important lesson to his people—that is, that unfaithfulness to his covenant will result in a break in their relationship with him that is just like the break in a relationship that occurs on divorce in a human marriage.

God the Husband of Israel

The Law of Marriage

But there is a deeper significance to the marital imagery, and to understand that, we need to understand an aspect of the Bible's marriage law recorded in Deuteronomy 24. The Old Testament prophets tell us that God uses this human marriage law to guide his own actions with Israel. It is found in Deuteronomy 24:

> When a man takes a wife and marries her, if then she finds no favour in his eyes because he has found some indecency in her, and he writes her a certificate of divorce and puts it in her hand and sends her out of his house, and she departs out of his house, and if she goes and becomes another man's wife, and the latter man hates her and writes her a certificate of divorce and puts it in her hand and sends her out of his house, or if the latter man dies, who took her to be his wife, then her former husband, who sent her away, may not take her again to be his wife, after she has been defiled, for that is an abomination before the LORD. And you shall not bring sin upon the land that the LORD your God is giving you for an inheritance. (Deuteronomy 24:1–4)

The "some indecency" of v. 1 is usually translated as sexual immorality. Thus, one aspect of this law is straight forward — sexual impurity by a wife permits a husband to divorce her, and Israel is warned in the marital imagery that God would divorce her if she was not faithful to him.

But this marriage law also binds a wife in two ways. Firstly, although she could divorce her husband, she could not go on to marry anybody else without the certificate which he alone could issue. Secondly, in whatever circumstance any subsequent marriage is terminated — death or divorce (with or without a certificate) — she could never remarry that first husband. This is despite there being no restrictions on her marrying other men. It is a strange "double lock" that gives an absolute prohibition on remarriage to the first husband in any circumstance. Scholars have puzzled over the reason for this and have given as many as ten possible explanations for it but (as others have pointed out) none of them are convincing.

The Bridegroom Messiah

The Law of Marriage Applied to Israel

When the prophets speak of "Israel" after the 722 BCE Assyrian exile, they are sometimes referring to the ten northern exiled tribes, but more usually they are referring to the two tribes from the south left behind, Judah and Benjamin—although they are sometimes referred to simply as "Judah."

As we have seen, Jeremiah describes Israel's Assyrian exile as a divorce, and in the passage below, explains that that means they cannot come back to God. He goes on to warn Judah that although *they* had not been divorced (they had not received the "decree of divorce"—the Deuteronomy 24 certificate), they should take note of Israel's predicament:

> If a man divorces his wife and she goes from him and becomes another man's wife, will he return to her? Would not that land be greatly polluted? [And yet] you have played the whore with many lovers; and would you return to me? declares the LORD ... The LORD said to me in the days of King Josiah: "Have you seen what she did, that faithless one, Israel, how she went up on every high hill and under every green tree, and there played the whore? And I thought, 'After she has done all this she will return to me', but she did not return, and her treacherous sister Judah saw it. She saw that for all the adulteries of that faithless one, Israel, I had sent her away with a decree of divorce. Yet her treacherous sister Judah did not fear, but she too went and played the whore. (Jeremiah 3:1, 6–8)

In the first verse Jeremiah points out the Deuteronomy law that states that once a divorced woman has become another man's wife the first husband cannot take her back. Jeremiah poses the rhetorical question to Judah: "If that happened to you Judah, will your first husband come back for you?" It demands the answer: "No, he cannot!" Jeremiah then goes on to say (vv. 6–8a) that this was Israel's fate. She had been sent away with her "decree of divorce" and so could not return. God is portrayed as being bound by his own marriage law. Jeremiah continues, "Yet her treacherous sister Judah did not fear, but she too went and played the whore" (v. 8b).

Jeremiah is saying that Judah should have feared the same fate as Israel and thus modified her behaviour, but she did not. He describes Judah as a wild animal lusting after many sexual encounters (2:23–25; 5:8); she has forgotten her husband (2:32–37); she has been unfaithful to him by whoring after other gods (2:27–28; 5:7); and has made alliances with other nations (2:36–37). As a consequence, Judah herself suffers exile in Babylon. But when despairing of her situation there, Isaiah seeks to comfort her:

> Thus says the LORD: "Where is your mother's certificate of divorce, with which I sent her away? Or which of my creditors is it to whom I have sold you? Behold, for your iniquities you were sold, and for your transgressions your mother was sent away." (Isaiah 50:1)

These are two more rhetorical questions: "When your parents' generation were sent away to Babylon were they given a certificate of divorce?" It demanded the answer: "No!" "And did God sell you to your creditors?" Again the expected answer is: "No!" Thus Isaiah held out a prospect of a return to God. Indeed, the Old Testament had repeatedly promised such a return—and not just for Judah, but for the whole of Israel.

A MARRIAGE IN EDEN

But before we come to the promise of a new future for Israel, to understand the full significance of the marriage law double lock, we need to reach further back in the Bible's story—to the garden of Eden and the creation of Adam and Eve. We know from that familiar story that God gave them a simple command—not to eat from the tree of the knowledge of good and evil (Genesis 2:17). And we know that, having been persuaded by Satan, it is the very thing they did.

But we might ask why, since God is complete in himself, did he create Adam and Eve in the first place? The events described after their disobedience shows that they had a relationship with God and talked directly with him:

> they heard the sound of the LORD God walking in the garden in the cool of the day, and the man and his wife hid themselves

The Bridegroom Messiah

> from the presence of the LORD God among the trees of the garden. But the LORD God called to the man and said to him, "Where are you?" And he said, "I heard the sound of you in the garden, and I was afraid, because I was naked, and I hid myself." He said, "Who told you that you were naked? Have you eaten of the tree of which I commanded you not to eat?" (Genesis 3:8–11)

The rest of the Bible story, as told by the marital imagery, makes it clear that it is this relationship between God and man that is central to man's creation. The meta-narrative of Scripture is the loss of that relationship, and its ultimate recovery at the marriage supper of the Lamb.

The 1646 Westminster Confession of Faith, influential in many churches worldwide, comments on the situation:

> By this sin, they [Adam and Eve] fell from their original righteousness and communion with God, and so became dead in sin, and wholly defiled in all the parts and faculties of soul and body. (Westminster Confession, 6.2)

And that subsequently all humanity is born with an intrinsically corrupt nature inherited from Adam and Eve:

> They [Adam and Eve] being the root of all mankind, the guilt of this sin was imputed, and the same death in sin and corrupted nature conveyed to all their posterity, descending from them by ordinary generation. (Westminster Confession, 6.3)

Thus, what happened is described as a "fall"—a term that implies that the first couple's disobedience caused them to fall from a state of perfection into a state of sin. The focus of that understanding is on what the Confession describes as a "loss of righteousness" and a "corrupt nature" being transmitted to mankind. It follows that the key problem for humanity is seen to be our relationship to Adam and the sinful nature we inherited from him. This perspective has dominated the Christian understanding of why Jesus came, and what it is he achieved on the cross. It is the lens through which we read the New Testament. However, the Bible does not use the word "fall," and

God the Husband of Israel

Anthony Thiselton has demonstrated the slender foundation in Scripture for the concepts that have become associated with this view.[ii]

The Bible's marital imagery uses a different perspective—its focus is on what the Confession describes as the loss of "communion with God." In the Edenic account, Satan is portrayed as an entity separate from the sin committed by Adam and Eve, and the Bible subsequently portrays this entity in various ways. For example, Genesis 4:7 says, "And if you do not do well, sin is crouching at the door. Its desire is for you, but you must rule over it"—here "sin" (i.e. Satan) is portrayed as a dangerous animal.

Similarly, the New Testament portrays "Sin" as somebody that can pay wages (Romans 6:23); and, as in Eden, we are told that Sin can lead you to sin (Romans 7:8); you can be imprisoned by Sin (Galatians 3:22); and can be freed from Sin (John 8:34–36); and the devil (Sin) is like a lion seeking someone to devour (1 Peter 5:8). To clarify the distinction between "Sin," and sins committed, I have capitalised "Sin" when sin is portrayed as an entity, or we might say, a "person."

The Bible's marital imagery takes up this personification of Sin and sees that it is possible to have a "relationship" with Sin. It is a relationship that Adam established when he did what Satan suggested. In so doing, Adam had repudiated his relationship with God and thus lost communion with him. In Genesis 3 we read the consequences of Adam's action:

> Therefore the LORD God sent him out from the garden of Eden to work the ground from which he was taken. He drove out the man, and at the east of the garden of Eden he placed the cherubim and a flaming sword that turned every way to guard the way to the tree of life. (Genesis 3:23–24)

Adam's fate is described here not as a fall, but rather as an exile. Or rather a "divorce"—the two Hebrew words translated as "sent" and "drove" in Genesis 3:23–24 are used elsewhere in the Old Testament to describe a divorce.[iii] We have seen that Israel is described as being in a "marital" relationship with God, and we read in Exodus 20 that God is a "jealous" God and Israel was to have "no other gods before me." In other words, Israel's relationship with God was to be an exclusive one—their failure in that duty led directly to their "divorce." The implication from the Edenic story is that God saw his relationship with Adam in similar terms—he expected covenant loyalty from Adam, just as in a human marriage. Adam's failure in that duty, just as with Israel, led to his own divorce.

Adam, in effect, took all mankind with him out of Eden—Adam's relationship with Satan had become all mankind's relationship with Satan. Nonetheless, the Bible's marital imagery does not portray the relationship with Adam as the problem—in the imagery, it is the relationship to Sin that is the root of mankind's problem.

An illustration might help see the significance of this different understanding. Your friend, Adam, takes you to a new restaurant where you get food poisoning and are ill for some time. It is true that Adam took you there—but the real problem is the food poisoning, not your relationship to Adam. Thus in the marital imagery, mankind's problem is their relationship with the "ruler of this world" (John 14:30, 2 Corinthians 4:4), and only indirectly because of their relationship with Adam.

Born Slaves

And that relationship with Adam, as the Westminster Confession says, is based on "ordinary generation." In other words, we are all in a "blood" relationship with Adam—he is the head of the whole human family. But rather than all mankind being born with a corrupted nature, the imagery suggests we are all born into the wrong relationship—that is, born, as Romans 6:6 describes, "slaves" of Sin.[iv] This is the theme of Romans 6, where the Roman believers are told that they were previously bound to Sin but were released by Christ's death to become "slaves" of righteousness (v. 20). It is because we are all born in a relationship with Sin that we all choose to do what Sin desires, it is thus no surprise that we all sin. In Romans 5:12 Paul puts it this way, "Therefore, just as sin came into the world through one man, and death through sin, and so death spread to all men because all sinned." This perspective is consonant with Jesus's comment that "everyone who practices sin is a slave to sin" (John 8:34).

Furthermore, this understanding suggests that when Paul speaks of the "body of sin" (Romans 6:6), he is not speaking of our corrupted mortal bodies, rather he is referring to those people that belong to Sin, as opposed to those people that belong to Christ (the "body of Christ"). So, while with both the Westminster Confession and the marital imagery understanding, the outcome of Adam's disobedience is the same—that is, that sin has polluted the whole of mankind, we will see that the imagery presents a different perspective to some New Testament teaching, and to the ultimate solution to man's dilemma— the cross. It is there that Jesus freed us from our relationship with Sin; John 8:36 tells us that, "if the Son sets you free [from Sin], you will be free indeed."

Adam and Israel Compared

But to return to our story, the problem for Israel was that they could not come back to God once they had gone with other "gods"—so it seems that Israel's story is a repeat of what had happened to Adam. Hosea 6:7 draws attention to that link, and their shared predicament: "But like Adam they [Israel] transgressed the covenant." Scholars have pointed out a great many other parallels between Adam and Israel, and that the Pentateuch deliberately draws attention to those parallels.[v]

We can layout the situation like this:

Adam is placed in a garden that will supply all his needs.	Israel is placed in the promised land, a land 'flowing with milk and honey.'
However, in the garden there was a serpent that caused Adam to sin.	However, in the land were the Canaanites who caused the Israelites to sin.

The Bridegroom Messiah

Adam was exiled from the garden. Genesis 3:23–24 uses two Hebrew words that mean divorce.	Israel was exiled from the land. Jeremiah 3:1–8 specifically describes it as a divorce.
Adam is not allowed to return (Genesis 3:24).	Israel is not allowed to return (Jeremiah 3:1–8).

Adam's story looks very much like a "pre-echo" of Israel's story. Israel could not go back to God because of the "law of marriage" that applies after a divorce (as Jeremiah explains) — Adam's exile is specifically spoken of as a divorce, and thus his predicament appears very much the same: he is excluded from Eden by God's own law of marriage.

The Deep Magic

C. S. Lewis portrays Adam's situation in his well-known allegorical Narnia stories. In *The Lion the Witch and the Wardrobe*, the Witch (Satan in the allegory) reminds Aslan (Jesus) of the "Deep Magic" of the "Emperor Beyond the Sea" (God the Father):

> You at least know the Magic which the Emperor put into Narnia at the very beginning. You know that every traitor belongs to me as my lawful prey and that for every treachery I have a right to a kill ... that human creature is mine. His life is forfeit to me. His blood is my property.[vi]

Edmund (Adam) — the "traitor" — belonged to the Witch, as Adamic humanity now belongs to Satan. The "Deep Magic" could only be broken by the death of Aslan. And so we read in Genesis 3:15, what has been described in church history as the *protoevangelium* (that is, the first statement of the Gospel):

> I will put enmity between you and the woman, and between your offspring and her offspring; he shall bruise your head, and you shall bruise his heel. (Genesis 3:15)

God the Husband of Israel

The key lesson from the Bible's marital imagery is that to free Adam from Satan's grasp, Christ was going to have to die to fulfil God's own law of marriage (the Deep Magic). Christ's battle is not to be primarily with *sins*, but with *Sin*. As our story unfolds I hope to show that this was the central purpose of the cross, and the essence of the gospel as told in the New Testament.

A PROMISED REMARRIAGE FOR ISRAEL

The Bible frequently promises a great future for Israel, and it is those promises we turn to now—promises that were often expressed as a future remarriage.

Hosea

Hosea 1:11 depicts a future reunion of Judah and Israel, and the statement, "they shall go up from the land" appears to be a prophecy of a future exodus. Hosea 2:14–15 follows that same theme suggesting a journey to a new promised land, but this time the "wilderness" does not represent a time of desolation, but rather a honeymoon, a time of intimacy devoid of distractions. Thus, Hosea is saying that the remarriage of God and Israel involves another exodus—a new exodus into a new promised land, and Hosea 2:16–23 refers to a new bridal time for God and his people. It is to be a completely new marriage, a new beginning.

Isaiah

Isaiah 54 also looks forward to a time of reconciliation. The reference to Israel's "widowhood" in v. 4 is probably a reference to Israel's deserted (v. 7), rather than bereaved, status. Verses 11–17 describe the reconciled Israel as a rebuilt Jerusalem. In contrast, Isaiah 61:10 speaks of Israel, in the first person singular, as being dressed like a bridegroom, and like a bride. Isaiah 62:1–8 also seems to refer to a remarriage of God and "Jerusalem."

Jeremiah

Jeremiah 3:18–22 similarly speaks of a reunited nation, and Jeremiah 31:31–32 specifically promises a new covenant, which is cited in Hebrews 8:8–13 as being mediated by Christ.

Ezekiel

In Ezekiel 40–44 God offers hope for the people, but the new "bride" is symbolised by a new Jerusalem, described as a temple city—the past has been left behind.

A Disappointed Judah

After 70 years of Babylonian exile Judah did indeed return—but it was not the triumphant return they expected. They came back to find that foreign powers controlled their home land, including the Romans, who eventually conquered Judea in 63 BCE. Judah quickly became dispirited and began, yet again, turning their backs on the things of God. Malachi comments on the situation:

> The oracle of the word of the LORD to Israel by Malachi. "I have loved you," says the LORD (Malachi 1:1–2)

Malachi is reminding Judah (Israel no longer exists as a nation) of God's past love for them. Then in Malachi 2:16 we read:

> "For I hate divorce," says the LORD, the God of Israel, "and him who covers his garment with wrong," says the LORD of hosts. "So take heed to your spirit, that you do not deal treacherously." (Malachi 2:16 NASB)

This is widely believed in the Christian community to be God giving his view on divorce in human marriage. But the Hebrew text is very unclear, and different translations give different versions of this verse. What is more, we need to consider the context of the statement. Malachi closes the "Book of the Twelve" (the twelve prophets from Hosea to Malachi at the end of our Old Testament were considered a single collection of books)—a "book" that opens with the marital imagery of Hosea—and Malachi's own opening statement is about God's declared love for wayward Judah. Also, God had given a specific command to the men of Judah through Ezra (who some think wrote Malachi) to divorce their foreign wives (Ezra 10:11). All these things suggest that God is speaking of his own coming divorce of Judah, and not (at least not here) criticising Jewish men for divorcing their wives. At the close of the book God holds out a promise, but he also gives a warning:

> Remember the law of my servant Moses, the statutes and rules that I commanded him at Horeb for all Israel. Behold, I will send you Elijah the prophet before the great and awesome day of the LORD comes. And he will turn the hearts of fathers to their children and the hearts of children to their fathers, lest I come and strike the land with a decree of utter destruction. (Malachi 4:4–6)

This is the situation as the Old Testament closes. Israel had already been divorced for their unfaithfulness to God, and we will see in the next chapter that Malachi's prophecy about Judah is fulfilled in the destruction of Jerusalem—it was God's final break with the people group he had covenanted with at Sinai.

A Glorious Remarriage

Nonetheless, we have seen the repeated remarriage prophecies in Hosea, Isaiah, Jeremiah, and Ezekiel. The old, Mosaic covenant was described as a marriage, so it was logical that any new covenant would be a new marriage. But those remarriage prophecies speak of the future in such glowing terms that the promised remarriage seems to indicate a totally new covenant—one that, as Jeremiah explains, is "not like" the old one (Jeremiah 31:31–32). But nobody knew what these prophecies meant in practice.

It is to that part of the story we now turn.

CHAPTER TWO

JESUS THE BRIDEGROOM MESSIAH

In the previous chapter we have seen some of the many promises of a future remarriage between God and his people. The Old Testament also contains a great many prophecies about a coming "Messiah" (in the Hebrew of the Old Testament, this word means the "anointed one"). This Messiah is described in various ways—he is to be a prophet like Moses (Deuteronomy 18:15–19), a priest like Melchizedek (Psalm 110:4), and a king like David (2 Sam 7:12–16; Psalm 2:6–8). We will see in this chapter that the early church and the New Testament writers understood Jesus Christ to be that Messiah, and that he came as God in the flesh to fulfil the Old Testament remarriage promises.

In the 400 years between the close of the Old Testament, and the beginning of the New Testament, there were raised expectations in Israel that the Messiah's arrival was imminent. They expected a great military leader to rescue them from the foreign powers that dominated their land. Israel would at last be vindicated and be seen to be the object of God's affection.

Thus it is perhaps understandable that many in Israel were reluctant to accept Jesus as the promised conqueror—he was the supposed illegitimate child of lowly birth who worked as a carpenter and spoke in his ministry of peace and love. Nonetheless, it became clear to the early believers that Jesus really was the Messiah the Old Testament spoke of. And so they came to call him Jesus the "anointed one," or Jesus the Christ (from *Christos*, the Greek for anointed)—or simply, Jesus Christ.

And although it seems that no one had been expecting the Messiah to be God in the flesh, the disciples eventually came to realise this. Thus, we have Thomas with his declaration, "My Lord and my God" (John 20:28); and John, when he says, "And we know that the Son of God has come ... He is the true God and eternal life." (1 John 5:20). But confusion persisted about *why* he came. Several disciples, as we will see, were still expecting a defeat of the Romans and a new future for national Israel.

I hope to show in the next chapters that the New Testament marital imagery provides a clear focus to both *why* Jesus came, and *who* he is.

JESUS IS THE BRIDEGROOM OF THE CHURCH

As the Gospels unfold their story it becomes clear that Jesus had come to fulfil the many Old Testament prophecies that described Israel's future. They included: a new exodus (Hosea 1:11; Hebrews 12:18–25); a reunited nation (Jeremiah 31:1; Hebrews 8:6); and a rebuilt Temple (Ezekiel 40–44; John 2:19–21). And for the Gentiles, those that were "not my people" would become "Children of the living God" (Hosea 1:10; Ephesians 2:11–16). We saw in our last chapter that all those Old Testament promises were framed within its marital imagery, as they are all to be fulfilled in a future new marriage. But Jeremiah 31 collects together many different Old Testament pictures that describe a glowing future for Israel—and, in effect, says that they are *all* to be fulfilled in the new covenant God promises. The book of Hebrews links that new covenant Jeremiah describes with the new covenant that Jesus mediates, a covenant that the New Testament makes clear is to be a new marriage. Hebrews 8, quoting from Jeremiah 31:31–32 (in italics as below), a chapter in which Jeremiah specifically describes God as Israel's husband, explains it like this:

> Christ has obtained a ministry that is as much more excellent than the old [covenant] as the covenant he mediates is better, since it is enacted on better promises. For if that first covenant had been faultless, there would have been no occasion to look for a second. For he finds fault with them when he says: *Behold, the days are coming, declares the Lord, when I will establish a new covenant with the house of Israel and with the house of Judah, not like the covenant that I made with their fathers on the day when I took them by the hand to bring them out of the land of Egypt. For they did not continue in my covenant, and so I showed no concern for them, declares the Lord.* (Hebrews 8:6–9)

The Bridegroom Messiah

Thus, all the new covenant promises relating to Israel's future are embraced in the new marital covenant—just as all the promises to ancient Israel (that is, a long life in a fruitful land) were contained in the old (Mosaic) marital covenant. We have seen that GOD IS THE HUSBAND OF ISRAEL was the conceptual metaphor that underpinned the Old Testament marital imagery. We will see in this chapter, that JESUS IS THE BRIDEGROOM OF THE CHURCH is the metaphor that underpins the New Testament marital imagery. The long-expected Messiah who is going to deliver on all those Old Testament promises is Jesus Christ. He is the Bridegroom Messiah.

Thus, the New Testament marital imagery consistently portrays the gospel invitation as an invitation to the wedding supper at the end of time when Jesus will take the church to himself as his bride. And throughout his ministry Jesus makes it clear that he is inviting all, Jew *and* Gentile, to believe in him and receive the offer of life. John 3:16 says: "For God so loved the world, that he gave his only Son, that whoever believes in him should not perish but have eternal life"—as Hosea 1:10 prophesied, those that are "not my people" will become "Children of the living God."

The Bridegroom Introduced

At the beginning of his ministry John the Baptist declared of Jesus:

> You yourselves bear me witness, that I said, "I am not the Christ, but I have been sent before him." The one who has the bride is the bridegroom. The friend of the bridegroom, who stands and hears him, rejoices greatly at the bridegroom's voice. Therefore this joy of mine is now complete. (John 3:28–29)

The reference to the "bridegroom's voice," is almost certainly a reference to Jeremiah 33:10–11, 14–17—verses that speak of God restoring Judah when, as Jeremiah explains, the voice of a bridegroom will be heard. And when John the Baptist describes himself as the "friend of the bridegroom," he is in effect comparing his role to that of the best man in a Jewish wedding, whose duty was to lead the bride to the bridegroom when the time for the wedding had arrived. John is making it clear that Jesus had come to make good on the Old Testament prophecies of a new marriage—a new covenant.

Jesus's Earthly Ministry is His Wedding Week

Philip Long has suggested that the whole of Jesus's earthly ministry is told in the synoptic Gospels as if it were the week before a Jewish wedding, and Jesus is the bridegroom to be.[vii] Certainly, all the Gospel writers use several contemporary marriage customs involving a bridegroom to describe Jesus's earthly ministry as a betrothal period. For example, when he was asked why his disciples were not fasting, Jesus answered:

> Can the wedding guests fast while the bridegroom is with them? As long as they have the bridegroom with them, they cannot fast. The days will come when the bridegroom is taken away from them, and then they will fast in that day. (Mark 2:19–20)

The Greek of the New Testament does not say "wedding guests," but rather "sons of the bride chamber." Contemporary records show that these were special friends of the bridegroom excused from religious duties for the wedding week celebration. So Jesus is comparing his three-and-a-half year earthly ministry before his death on the cross to that week.

Jesus and the Wedding in Cana

In John 2:1–11, when at the wedding in Cana, Mary commented to Jesus on the shortfall of wine. It seems that at Jewish weddings it was the bridegroom's responsibility to provide the wine (as inferred in v. 9). This probably accounts for Jesus's reply to her, "Woman, what does this have to do with me? My hour is not yet come" (v. 4). Mary had been, in effect, asking Jesus to prematurely declare himself as the messianic bridegroom. However, a short time later Jesus declared to the Samaritan woman, "But the hour is coming, and is now here, when the true worshipers will worship the Father in spirit and truth, for the Father is seeking such people to worship him" (John 4:23).

But in John 13:1, Jesus's "hour" is associated not with the beginning of his ministry, but the end. We read, "Now before the Feast of the Passover, when Jesus knew that his hour had come to depart out of this world to the Father." The Gospels (for example Luke 22:14–23) describe the situation, and 1 Corinthians 11:25 says:

> In the same way also he took the cup, after supper, saying, "This cup is the new covenant in my blood. Do this, as often as you drink it, in remembrance of me."

Thus, the Last Supper is linked to the new marriage covenant promised to Israel by God in Jeremiah 31:31–33 where he speaks of being a husband in a new covenant. In effect, the Last Supper is Jesus's own wedding banquet, and the twelve disciples represent Jesus's bride, the church.

The parable of the ten virgins in Matthew 25:1–13 similarly uses marital imagery to portray the situation at the end of time. In New Testament times, weddings climaxed with the arrival of the bridegroom at the wedding feast—thus the parable portrays Jesus's unexpected arrival as the bridegroom at his own wedding. In the final chapter we will look at more examples of marital imagery in the New Testament that have been drawn from contemporary Jewish marriage traditions to illustrate aspects of the cross.

THE BRIDEGROOM MESSIAH IS GOD IN THE FLESH

Jesus Provides What God Said He Himself Would Provide

We have seen how in John 2:1–11, when at the wedding in Cana, Mary commented to Jesus on the shortfall of wine and Jesus's reply to her, "Woman, what does this have to do with me? My hour is not yet come" (v. 4). Despite this comment, Jesus nonetheless did as his mother had requested and performed the miracle. When the wine is produced, the master of the feast comments on its quality and assumes it is the bridegroom who has made the provision (vv. 9–10). Many of the readers of John's Gospel would know the book of Isaiah very well and would not have missed the significance of this miracle. Verses 7, 9, and 11 of Isaiah 24 refer to a lack of wine when Israel was suffering from the Assyrian invasion. But in the next chapter Isaiah describes a future restoration when God will ensure wine will be in abundance (Isaiah 25:6–8). Isaiah said it was God himself who was going to provide, "a feast of well-aged wine"—now Jesus had done exactly that. It seems clear that Jesus is showing the wedding guests, and through John showing us, that he is God in the flesh, come as the promised Bridegroom Messiah, and that the time for the promised restoration, and a new start, had at last come.

Jesus Offers the Remarriage to Israel That God Had Promised

In John 4:1–29 we have the story of the woman from Samaria. The first ten verses set the scene:

> Now when Jesus learned that the Pharisees had heard that Jesus was making and baptizing more disciples than John (although Jesus himself did not baptize, but only his disciples), he left Judea and departed again for Galilee. And he had to pass through Samaria. So he came to a town of Samaria called Sychar, near the field that Jacob had given to his son Joseph. Jacob's well was there; so Jesus, wearied as he was from his journey, was sitting beside the well. It was about the sixth hour. There a woman from Samaria came to draw water. Jesus said to her, "Give me a drink." (For his disciples had gone away into the city to buy food.) The Samaritan woman said to him, "How is it that you, a Jew, ask for a drink from me, a woman of Samaria?" (For Jews have no dealings with Samaritans.) Jesus answered her, "If you knew the gift of God, and who it is that is saying to you, 'Give me a drink,' you would have asked him, and he would have given you living water." (John 4:1–10)

I suggest that in this encounter, Jesus is treating this woman not just as an individual, but as a symbol for her people, and presenting himself as a bridegroom and offering to her a "marriage"—in other words, inviting both her, and the despised Samaritans, to come to God.

The Bridegroom Messiah

There are clear connections in this story with previous meetings at a well that resulted in marriage (Isaac and Rebekah, Genesis 24:14–16; Jacob and Rachel, Genesis 29:1–20; Moses and Zipporah, Exodus 2:15–17, 21). There are so many detailed parallels (particularly with Jacob and Rachel's meeting at a well recorded in Genesis 29) that only a few can be mentioned. For example, John portrays Jesus, just like Jacob, as a man from another a country, seeking a bride, arriving at a well at the middle of the day, and asking a single woman for a drink, who on realising the man's identity, ran home to tell her people. What is more, Jacob is specifically referenced no fewer than three times in the account in John 4.

We will confine ourselves to just a few aspects of the passage to demonstrate how, in this encounter, Jesus identified himself as both the Bridegroom Messiah and God in the flesh. In v. 10 Jesus says, "If you knew the gift of God, and who it is that is saying to you, 'Give me a drink,' you would have asked him, and he would have given you living water." Jesus turns the conversation from literal water to spiritual matters, and in this context the term "living water" seems to have bridal associations—referring to the ritual bath a Jewish bride took before her wedding. Indeed, in the Old Testament, in the Song of Solomon 4:12, 15, there is a link with a bride and living water: "A garden locked is my sister, my bride, a spring locked, a fountain sealed … a garden fountain, a well of living water."

It might be thought that the passage would never have been understood this way by the Samaritan woman, or by any readers of John's account at the time he wrote it. But I believe it can be demonstrated that the Samaritan woman did indeed understand what Jesus was saying, and that it is likely that the contemporary readers would have done so as well.

In first century Palestine, if a young man wanted to meet a young woman the well was the best place to go—as we have mentioned, Moses, Isaac, and Jacob all met their wives there. Jesus, a single man, was alone with this woman, a place where you go to meet a potential marriage partner, and this might explain the reaction of the disciples when they came back and found him there (v. 27). What is more, it is

Jesus the Bridegroom Messiah

Jesus himself who introduces the marital theme when he asks her to bring her husband (vv. 16–18). Some think Jesus wants to point out the woman's dubious marital history, but this does not fit the redemptive theme of the encounter. Furthermore, notwithstanding her latest relationship, just as in Roman Catholic England when the pious Catherine Parr (the last wife of Henry VIII) had married four husbands, there is nothing to suggest that in Israel to have had five husbands was in any way sinful.

The religious context also supports an interpretation that a wider issue was being addressed. The Samaritan people were the remnants of the northern tribes of Israel that had been "divorced" by God— Samaria had been the home of Ephraim when the Assyrians invaded; some had stayed, but others were deported to Assyria. Although many subsequently returned, in the process there had been much intermarrying with foreigners—the Samaritans were now a mixture of Jewish and Gentile blood and no longer considered "Jewish" by their Jewish neighbours. What is more, they embraced a religion that was a mixture of Judaism and idolatry. They worshipped the true God, but they also had a history of involvement with the cults of five different nations—these were referred to as the five false gods of Samaria, as demonstrated by Josephus in his writings. The Canaanite word for a god is Baal, the same word sometimes used for "husband" in the Hebrew Bible (Hosea making a wordplay on it in Hosea 2:16, "And in that day, declares the LORD, you will call me 'My Husband,' and no longer will you call me 'My Baal.'"). The fact that the Samaritans worshipped the true God, but also had a history of worshipping these five false gods, was well known. The Old Testament account of them is found in 2 Kings 17:24–34. Verses 33–34 summarise the situation:

> So they feared the LORD but also served their own gods, after the manner of the nations from among whom they had been carried away. To this day they do according to the former manner. They do not fear the LORD, and they do not follow the statutes or the rules or the law or the commandment that the LORD commanded the children of Jacob, whom he named Israel. (2 Kings 17: 33–34)

The Bridegroom Messiah

The Samaritans had an outward appearance of fearing the LORD in their worship, but in reality, they did not fear him at all as they did not keep his commands. Thus, the Jews looked down on them because of their mixed blood, their false gods, and the fact they had their own temple on Mount Gerizim which, however, the Samaritans insisted was designated by Moses as the place where the nation should worship. In summary, there were two issues relating to their worship—the five false gods, and the true God the Samaritans worshipped, but at the wrong temple.

I suggest that all these things are key to Jesus's conversation with this woman at the well. Jesus was steadily moving to the point he wanted to make—he is the Messiah, the Saviour of Jew, Gentile, and even of the Samaritans. He is the Christ who is going to sweep away the idea that God could only be worshipped in one particular place. Jesus points to her five husbands (five false gods), and the fact that the man she is presently co-habiting with is not her husband. This last relationship was wrong, and thus an analogy automatically arises from this sixth "husband," to the Samaritan worship of the true God (the sixth "god"), but at the wrong temple.

If we look at the relevant section from our passage in John 4, vv. 16–20, most commentators say that the woman at this point changes the topic to speak of religious things so as to divert Jesus away from her private life. But the woman, I believe, makes it clear that she had understood exactly what Jesus was saying. In her reply to him at v. 19, immediately after acknowledging Jesus's supernatural knowledge of her private life ("Sir, I perceive that you are a prophet"), goes directly to speak of that temple (her sixth "god"): "Our fathers worshiped on this mountain, but you say that in Jerusalem is the place where people ought to worship." Jesus, the master evangelist, with the illustration from her private life, had brought her to the precise point he wanted—to show that now the promised Christ had come the temples at Gerizim and Jerusalem were of no consequence, and what is more the Jew/Gentile division had ended, as Jesus clearly implies in vv. 21–26.

Jesus the Bridegroom Messiah

In this conversation with Jesus, the woman is serving as a symbol for lost northern Israel, just as had Hosea's wife, Gomer, in a previous century. Jesus is offering the woman, and through her, the Samaritan people (divorced Israel), in this traditional Jewish setting for betrothals, redemption in a new marriage. The Roman Catholic scholar, Brant Pitre, says, "through this encounter with Jesus the non-Jewish peoples of the world begin to be betrothed—so to speak—to the one who is both Bridegroom Messiah and Savior of the world."

John tells us:

> Just then his disciples came back. They marvelled that he was talking with a woman, but no one said, "What do you seek?" or, "Why are you talking with her?" So the woman left her water jar and went away into town and said to the people, "Come, see a man who told me all that I ever did. Can this be the Christ?" (John 4:27–29)

It seems that the woman had realised the full significance of what Jesus had said, and went to tell not her family, or her household, but "the people." Who were "the people?" They were the Samaritans. But tell them what? Her focus was not her personal salvation. She said, "Come, see a man who told me all the things that I have done" (v. 29 NASB). She was amazed at Jesus's prophetic knowledge of her marital history, but I suggest even more than that, she was amazed by his declaration of the abolition of the Jew/Gentile division. Could it be that the gist of her message was: "Can this be the Christ? If so, can it be that he has come for us, even us, whom the Jews despise?"

Isaiah says:

> For your Maker is your husband, the LORD of hosts is his name; and the Holy One of Israel is your Redeemer, the God of the whole earth he is called. For the LORD has called you like a wife deserted and grieved in spirit, like a wife of youth when she is cast off, says your God. For a brief moment I deserted you, but with great compassion I will gather you. (Isaiah 54:5–7)

The Bridegroom Messiah

Isaiah is telling us that it is God himself who will come for Israel and be the husband. And Hosea specifically says that this future involves both Israel (now the Samaritans) and Judah:

> Yet the number of the children of Israel shall be like the sand of the sea, which cannot be measured or numbered. And in the place where it was said to them, "You are not my people," it shall be said to them, "Children of the living God." And the children of Judah and the children of Israel shall be gathered together, and they shall appoint for themselves one head. And they shall go up from the land, for great shall be the day of Jezreel. (Hosea 1:10–11)

"Jezreel" is another wordplay by Hosea (as in Hosea 2:16)—in Hebrew it looks and sounds just like "Israel." It was God who had married Israel, God who had divorced her, and it is the same God who promises a remarriage—it is a glorious future for "Jezreel."

We can see from this encounter with the Samaritan woman that Jesus does not speak as a messenger. He does not say to her: "Go to God, he is ready to be reconciled to you, and to your people, in fulfilment of his long-promised remarriage." Instead Jesus says to her, and to others in the Gospel narratives: "Come to me." Many theologians since the 19th century have suggested that the early church read the divinity of Christ back into the New Testament, and that Jesus himself did not think he was God. But as we can see, the Gospel writers portray Jesus in his ministry as self-consciously taking on the role of the Bridegroom Messiah, and this imagery is tightly bound into the Gospel story—it could not be a later addition.

The Bridegroom Messiah Declares the Divorce of Judah

We saw in the last chapter that Judah, even though sent away to Babylon, God did not divorce her; even so, the closing verses of Malachi contained the warning that unless she changed her ways the land would be struck with "utter destruction." John the Baptist, the promised "Elijah" of Malachi 4, declared to his audience:

> And do not presume to say to yourselves, "We have Abraham as our father," for I tell you, God is able from these stones to raise up children for Abraham. Even now the axe is laid to the root of the trees. Every tree therefore that does not bear good fruit is cut down and thrown into the fire. (Matthew 3:9–10)

But the change of heart that Malachi tells us that God was looking for did not occur, and Jesus towards the end of his ministry looks across at Jerusalem, and in Matthew 23 (also Luke 13:34–35) makes this comment:

> O Jerusalem, Jerusalem, the city that kills the prophets and stones those who are sent to it! How often would I have gathered your children together as a hen gathers her brood under her wings, and you would not! See, your house is left to you desolate. For I tell you, you will not see me again, until you say, "Blessed is he who comes in the name of the Lord." (Matthew 23:37–39)

A similar lesson seems to be taught in the parable of the king's banquet. Although Jesus is not portrayed as the bridegroom, rather as a king, it is nonetheless clear that the parable describes Jesus's own ministry as inviting people to a wedding feast—but some refused:

> The kingdom of heaven may be compared to a king who gave a wedding feast for his son, and sent his servants to call those who were invited to the wedding feast, but they would not come. Again he sent other servants, saying, "Tell those who are invited, See, I have prepared my dinner, my oxen and my fat calves have been slaughtered, and everything is ready. Come to the wedding feast." But they paid no attention and went off, one to his farm, another to his business, while the rest seized his servants, treated them shamefully, and killed them. The king was angry, and he sent his troops and destroyed those murderers and burned their city. (Matthew 22:2–7)

The teaching of the parable appears to be that Israel rejected the Bridegroom Messiah's wedding invitation, and were in turn rejected by the Messiah. The parable of the tenants of the vineyard who beat the servants of the owner (e.g. Matthew 21:33–46), and the fig tree that gave no fruit (Luke 13:6–9), convey a similar message.[viii]

So even though the word often translated as divorce (*apolysē*) does not specifically appear in any of these passages, in light of the pervasive marital imagery of the New Testament, it seems clear that Jesus is speaking of the final divorce of the people God had taken to himself at Sinai. The destruction by the Romans in 70 CE of Jerusalem and its temple symbolised this divorce. To be present at the remarriage the Old Testament prophets spoke of, and claim the promise of a new heavens and earth, any blood descendants of Jacob will have to go in faith to the Bridegroom Messiah. The temple, which for Jewish people had been the centre of worship, has never been rebuilt.

IN SUMMARY

We know from Scripture teaching that a man can only betroth a single, widowed, or divorced woman, never a *married* woman—such would be adulterous (Exodus 20:14). The imagery of Jesus as the bridegroom seeking his bride (not as the reconciling husband seeking his estranged wife) that is integral to the New Testament assumes a divorced Israel. We read in John 1:11 that Jesus "came to his own, and his own people did not receive him"—he came for Israel, but as a people group they rejected him.

Thus, Jesus came to offer all, divorced Israel, separated (but soon to be divorced) Judah, and the Gentiles ("divorced" at Eden), a place at his own wedding supper, the wedding supper of the Lamb. In so doing he clearly demonstrated that he is the promised Messiah—the Bridegroom Messiah, God in the flesh.

In the next chapter we will look at the new covenant Jesus came to inaugurate. It is a covenant foreshadowed in God's first recorded words to Satan after he had tempted Adam and Eve into their disastrous choice. A choice that caused them, and all mankind, to be banished from the presence of God.

Jesus the Bridegroom Messiah

In the final chapter we will see how Jesus overcame the Deuteronomy 24 law of marriage with its double lock (Lewis's Deep Magic)—a law that would have prevented him, as God in the flesh, taking back the wife he had divorced.

CHAPTER THREE

THE NEW COVENANT

Jesus told his disciples at the last supper that he had come to inaugurate a new covenant and that his death was the means to that end: "And likewise the cup after they had eaten, saying, 'This cup that is poured out for you is the new covenant in my blood'" (Luke 22:20). But just before his ascension they asked of him, "Lord, will you at this time restore the kingdom to Israel?" (Acts 1:6)—it seems that they were still expecting a literal, and specifically Jewish, fulfilment of the many Old Testament Messianic prophecies.

And subsequent events in the early church demonstrate that there was some difficulty coming to terms with just how different the old and new covenants were, and in understanding the relationship between the two. Examples include the Jerusalem Council discussions in Acts 15, and the issues that Paul highlights in his letter to the Galatians. This problem has persisted in church history. We have seen that some of the great 16th century Reformers taught that the old and new covenants are fundamentally the same, and the discussion about this in the church continues to our own day. It is beyond the scope of this chapter to look at this in any detail but further consideration is given to it in Some Reflections at the end of the book.

Instead, I hope to briefly show in this chapter that the marital imagery demonstrates that the new covenant is indeed new. And that Jesus's death on the cross was to fulfil God's mysterious law of marriage, and thus enable the Bridegroom Messiah to take the elect directly into the Abrahamic promise of a blessing to "all the nations" and the new marriage that the Old Testament speaks of.

THE NEW COVENANT IS NEW

We will see that while the old covenant points to the new covenant, the source of the new covenant is not found in the old covenant. Paul specifically tells us this:

The New Covenant

> But now the righteousness of God has been manifested apart from the [Mosaic] law, although the Law and the Prophets [all the Old Testament] bear witness to it. (Romans 3:21)

He is saying that there has now been revealed a way to get right with God apart from the Mosaic law—in other words, there is a *different* way: "The righteousness of God [is] through faith in Jesus Christ for all who believe" (Romans 3:22). The Mosaic covenant, with its 600 plus law codes, was made obsolete, as Hebrews 8:13 points out: "In speaking of a new covenant, he makes the first one obsolete. And what is becoming obsolete and growing old is ready to vanish away."

The book of Hebrews was written after Jesus's death but before the destruction of the Jerusalem. We are told in v. 13 that the old covenant is "ready to vanish away"—thus at the time that Hebrews was written, this had not yet happened. The Mosaic covenant is, however, finally terminated when the temple, the "heart" of that covenant, is razed to the ground in 70 CE. It seems clear from this that Jesus's death was not to terminate the old covenant, but to inaugurate the new covenant—as he had told his disciples.

An illustration might help us understand the relationship between the two covenants. A few years ago, contractors were employed to build a new road from the village where I live to the adjacent village about two kilometres away. The old road, with its stone bridge crossing the river, was left in place. However, some local residents continued to use it, often insisting (as is the way with these things) that it was the best route. Some years later, because the old stone bridge was considered unsafe, the local council closed the road.

And so it is that the new covenant did not "close" the old covenant, any more than our new road closed the old road. The old covenant was made obsolete by the new covenant, and that old covenant was subsequently terminated by the divorce Jesus prophesied in Matthew 23 and Luke 13. In this way God made it clear that the Mosaic covenant, with its hundreds of written law codes, was no longer the way to approach God.

The Bridegroom Messiah

To continue with our illustration, the new road to our adjacent village was not based on the old road—it really was new. It started at a different place, it employed a different technology (including a wide span steel and concrete bridge), and ended at a different place. Similarly, as we will see below, although the old and new covenants are connected in purpose (just as our old road and new roads were), they are fundamentally different. Firstly, the new covenant starts not in the desert at Sinai, or even with a promise to Abraham, but in the garden of Eden. Secondly, as we shall see shortly, it employs a different "technology"—a faith-based affinity union with the Bridegroom Messiah, Abraham's distant seed, not a blood union with his grandson Jacob. And thirdly, its destination is different. The Mosaic covenant took Israel to an earthly land where the presence of God was mediated by prophets and priests. In contrast, the new covenant takes the church into the very presence of God in a new heavens and new earth.

THE NEW COVENANT STARTS IN EDEN

The Promise to Abraham and the Seed of Genesis 3:15

In the Genesis account, immediately before Adam's expulsion from the Garden of Eden, we read these words from God addressed to Satan:

> I will put enmity between you and the woman, and between your offspring and her offspring; he shall bruise your head, and you shall bruise his heel. (Genesis 3:15)

Paul references this verse when he tells the Roman believers that, "The God of peace will soon crush Satan under your feet" (Romans 16:20). It is clear that Paul sees that the seed of the woman, the God of peace, and the Lord Jesus Christ, are all one and the same. God's words are the *protoevangelium* we referred to in chapter one—the foreshadowing of the gospel. The promise of the defeat of Satan, and an eventual return into God's presence, is the gospel that Jesus came to proclaim and fulfil. We will see that this promise is central both to the new covenant and Christ's work on the cross.

The New Covenant

Many years later, but still more than 400 years before the Mosaic covenant with Israel, God promised to Abraham that he will be the father of a great nation. It is a promise repeated several times in Genesis 12–17. But then in Genesis 22 we read:

> "I will surely bless you, and I will surely multiply your offspring as the stars of heaven and as the sand that is on the seashore. And your offspring shall possess the gate of his enemies, and in your offspring shall all the nations of the earth be blessed, because you have obeyed my voice." (Genesis 22:17–18)

The Origin of the New Covenant Foreseen

The promises to Abraham certainly included the nation descended from Abraham's grandson Jacob (who was renamed Israel), a nation that eventually entered the "promised land"—that is, the land that was promised to Abraham. However, in his letter to the Galatians Paul makes it clear that this particular promise in Genesis 22 foreshadowed the gospel:

> And the Scripture, foreseeing that God would justify the Gentiles by faith, preached the gospel beforehand to Abraham, saying, "In you shall all the nations be blessed." (Galatians 3:8)

He continues by explaining that there was another aspect to the literal nation promises given to Abraham, arguing that "offspring" in Genesis 22:17–18 is a reference to Jesus Christ.

> Now the promises were made to Abraham and to his offspring. It does not say, "And to offsprings," referring to many, but referring to one, "And to your offspring," who is Christ. This is what I mean: the law [the Mosaic covenant], which came 430 years afterward, does not annul a covenant previously ratified by God, so as to make the promise void. (Galatians 3:16–17)

Scholars have pointed out that the "offspring" (or "seed" as it is in NIV) in both Genesis 3:15 and Genesis 22:17, in the Hebrew text itself, is intended to be understood as a single seed.[ix] So Paul is not stretching the understanding of the original promise to Abraham to make his point, which is that the text is referring to the promised Messiah. (He employs the same argument in Romans 4:13–25, but his focus there is on the *contrast* between the fulfilment of the literal nation promise compared to that of the "all the nations" single seed promise.) G. K. Beale comments:

> there are no clear examples where they [the New Testament writers] have developed a meaning from the Old Testament which is inconsistent or contradictory to some aspect of the original Old Testament intention.[x]

So, while Paul does not deny a literal nation fulfilment, he explains that there were, in effect, *two* promises given to Abraham (or at least two aspects to the one promise), one fulfilled in Jacob and his many descendants who God covenanted with at Sinai, and another that lay in the more distant future with a very specific offspring—that is Jesus Christ. This promise of a second specific seed might have been somewhat hidden in that original promise, Paul himself indicating such when he says in Galatians 3:8, "Scripture foreseeing that God would justify the Gentiles by faith." In other words, Scripture foresaw it rather than Abraham.

But nonetheless Paul clarifies that the Genesis 22:18 "all the nations" promise demonstrates that it was always God's intention that all the nations of the earth would be blessed by a single seed whose arrival lay in the more distant future. This seed is, of course, Jesus Christ. Thus, Jesus would be descended from Abraham, as was Jacob.

So Paul directly links the *protoevangelium* of Genesis 3:15 with the Genesis 22:17–18 Abrahamic promise. Furthermore, as we see above, in Galatians 3:16–17 Paul points out that the old covenant does not annul the separate earlier promise of the Saviour. In other words, the promise of the Saviour was not dependent on, or impacted by, the Mosaic covenant. The promise of a blessing to all nations through Jesus Christ stands on its own.

The New Covenant

It is perhaps helpful at this point to distinguish between a promise and a covenant—a covenant can be thought of as a promise crystallised. The Mosaic covenant crystallised the promise to Abraham of a literal physical nation and land. But there was to be another seed of Abraham, one particular seed, that would form the basis of another, different covenant, that was to be 'not like' the old covenant (Jeremiah 31:32). The New Testament makes it clear that those who could lay a claim to *this* seed, would gain not an earthly kingdom, but a spiritual one. In other words, there was a promised seed that inherited an earthly kingdom (Israel), but another seed, Jesus Christ, would offer "an inheritance that is imperishable, undefiled, and unfading, kept in heaven for you" (1 Peter 1:4).

Jesus Christ came to inaugurate the new covenant that crystallises the future seed promise God had made to Abraham. It is a promise that is rooted in the Genesis 3:15 prophecy of a spiritual battle with evil to reverse the effects of the banishment from Eden. It is a battle to the death, which the Saviour will win, but at great personal cost.

THE NEW COVENANT HAS A NEW AFFINITY BASIS

But how can the Gentiles, who by definition are not of Abraham's seed, lay claim to either promise? The answer is that the new covenant works on a different basis to that of the old covenant. That old Mosaic covenant was based on a blood line—all those descended from Abraham via Jacob were automatically included in the covenant. In contrast, we will see that the new covenant basis is found in Genesis 2:24, and thus key to understanding that covenant is understanding that verse. However, it seems that historically the unanimous view in the Christian church has been that Genesis 2:24 is a reference to Adam and Eve as described in Genesis 2:23. The two verses say:

> [23] Then the man said, "This at last is bone of my bones and flesh of my flesh; she shall be called Woman, because she was taken out of Man." [24] Therefore a man shall leave his father and his mother and hold fast to his wife, and they shall become one flesh.

The Bridegroom Messiah

The Old Testament was written in Hebrew and it is possible to get the wrong impression from many of our modern English translations of Genesis 2:24 that use "therefore" and "one flesh." An equally valid translation, and one that would more accurately convey its original meaning, would be:

> After that [i.e. in *contrast* to Adam and Eve], a man shall leave his father and his mother and hold fast to his wife, and they shall become one family.

This is certainly how the verse was understood in Old Testament times.[xi] If we look at the two verses in light of this, we can see that both Adam and Eve were miraculously created by God—their formation and union were part of the sequence of events when God created the world, after which he "rested" (Genesis 2:23). In contrast, Genesis 2:24 seems to be a reference to the ordinary cycle of life, speaking of naturally born men and women, and a man leaving his father and mother to join his wife. In this marriage, the couple *become* "one flesh"—in other words, something has changed.

This contrasts with Adam and Eve who always were the same flesh– literally! This fact seems to be confirmed by the Hebrew, in that it says in Genesis 2:23 that Eve came *from* Adam, but in Genesis 2:24 it says that the married couple come *into* their relationship. Furthermore, the Genesis 2:24 union is formed by the couple themselves, they choose each other. By way of contrast, for Adam and Eve, there was no choice. Their union was formed by God.

We can set the differences out between the two marriages like this:

The New Covenant

Genesis 2:23	Genesis 2:24
1. A miraculous man and woman.	1. A naturally born man and woman.
2. Remain as they are.	2. Choose to become what they were not.
3. In a literal one-flesh blood union.	3. In a marital affinity relationship forming a new family unit.
4. Without the need for a covenant.	4. By means of their marriage vows—their covenant.

Thus Genesis 2:24 is a marital *affinity* union—quite unlike the blood union of the first couple described in Genesis 2:23, where Eve literally was "one flesh" with Adam. We see this distinction in families with birth children. I did not need a covenant with my children for them to be my children—they were born to my wife and myself, whereas my wife chose to become what she was not, a member of my family by means of our marriage covenant, symbolised in her changing her family name to my family name. We might say that she is now *counted as* a Hamer, although born a Jackman.

With this in mind, we can now see that Paul reveals in his letter to the Ephesians how the Abrahamic gospel promise of a spiritual kingdom of many nations is going to be achieved. He points out the dilemma for the Gentiles:

> Therefore remember that at one time you Gentiles in the flesh, called "the uncircumcision" by what is called the circumcision, which is made in the flesh by hands—remember that you were at that time separated from Christ, alienated from the commonwealth of Israel and strangers to the covenants of promise, having no hope and without God in the world. (Ephesians 2:11–12)

In the letter, Paul keeps calling the promised inclusion of the Gentiles in God's plan a "mystery," for example, in Ephesians 3:6: "This mystery is that the Gentiles are fellow heirs, members of the same body and partakers of the promise in Christ Jesus through the gospel" — in fact by the time Paul gets to chapter 5 he has declared it a mystery no fewer than five times (Ephesians 1:9; 3:3, 4, 6, 9). And then he says:

> "Therefore a man shall leave his father and mother and hold fast to his wife, and the two shall become one flesh." This mystery is profound, and I am saying that it refers to Christ and the church. (Ephesians 5:31–32)

Paul is saying that the mystery, that is, the inclusion of the Gentiles, is based on the fact that "Genesis 2:24 = Christ and the church." With our understanding of Genesis 2:24 it is clear that Paul is saying that Jesus's bridal community is to be formed by those people who, although outside of Abraham's family, can *choose* to become, by faith, what they are not (albeit drawn by the Holy Spirit as John 6:44 explains), that is, members of Jesus's bridal community—the church.

We know that the bridegroom of the church is Jesus Christ. And as we have seen Paul, in Galatians 3:16, tells us that he is also the promised seed of Abraham. It follows that the whole church is in a marital affinity relationship with the seed of Abraham—and thus can be *counted as* being in his family. Paul, under the inspiration of God, shows how Genesis 2:24 foreshadows the gospel, in that it is the Genesis 2:24 marital affinity relationship that brings the Gentiles into the promised all nations "family" of Abraham.

In contrast, if we look at national Israel, although they, as a nation, became what they were not, the bride of God, at Sinai—subsequently each individual Jew came into that bridal community without choice, and without a change of status. This is rather like Eve, who was "born" into her marital relationship with Adam as recorded in Genesis 2:23—she came *from* Adam just as a Jew comes *from* Abraham.

But the church is based on Genesis 2:24 principles, and these embrace the concept of each individual making a choice to come *into* a relationship with the seed of Abraham. The Gentiles, unlike the descendants of Jacob, are born outside of any relationship with God, but can nonetheless now come into the Abrahamic family and thus into the promise God gave him. The two covenants operate in a fundamentally different way—one based on the concept of a Genesis 2:23 union, the other based on a Genesis 2:24 union. It is a clash of concepts that runs through the New Testament.

John Highlights the Faith and Blood Contrast

John in his Gospel highlights the difference between the affinity union of the new covenant that is to be based on faith, and the blood line of the old covenant, in his very first chapter:

> Yet to all who did receive him, to those who believed in his name, he gave the right to become children of God—children born not of natural descent, nor of human decision or a husband's will, but born of God. (John 1:12–13 NIV)

The old covenant was based on the natural descent—that is, the blood line from Jacob. Children were born into that bridal community by a human decision. Or more specifically, as John says, by "a husband's will"—that is, the will of the Jewish husband who chose to conceive a child with his wife thus bringing that child automatically into the Mosaic covenant. In contrast, John is saying that Jesus gave the right to become the children of God to those that believed in him. It was not a matter of the circumstances of your birth, as it had been under the old covenant. And then in chapter 3, John goes further and says this:

> That which is born of the flesh is flesh, and that which is born of the Spirit is spirit. (John 3:6)

Those born "of the flesh" into the Mosaic covenant were promised, conditional on staying within the covenant conditions, a long earthly life in a physical land (e.g. Exodus 20:12; Deuteronomy 6:1–2; 30:17–20). So although it was a covenant that *foreshadowed* a heavenly covenant, *in and of itself* it was earthly, not heavenly. In contrast, those that are born of the Holy Spirit, come by faith into their eternal bridal community—into a kingdom that is "not of this world" (John 18:36). In other words, John 3:6 is saying that the old covenant was not a covenant that gave you spiritual life—for that you had to go to Christ.

The Bridegroom Messiah

In light of John's comment, it seems that when Paul says in Galatians 3:11 that, "no one is justified before God by the [Mosaic] law," he does not mean that Israel (or anybody else) failed to reach the goal—but rather that the law could *never* have given spiritual life. For spiritual life, you had to come into the Abrahamic promised blessing via Jesus Christ, his promised spiritual seed. But of course, Israel had not seen it this way, and thus we get the extended exchange about this between Jesus and the Pharisees in John 8. We read there that Jesus first explains that everyone is a slave to Sin:

> "Truly, truly, I say to you, everyone who practices sin is a slave to sin. The slave does not remain in the house forever; the son remains forever. So if the Son sets you free, you will be free indeed." (John 8:34 –36)

And that this included Jewish people:

> "I know that you are offspring of Abraham; yet you seek to kill me because my word finds no place in you. I speak of what I have seen with my Father, and you do what you have heard from your father." They answered him, "Abraham is our father." Jesus said to them, "If you were Abraham's children, you would be doing the works Abraham did … You are of your father the devil." (John 8:37–39, 44)

Jesus makes it clear that being descended by blood from Abraham, and thus automatically included in the Mosaic covenant, does not mean automatic inclusion in the kingdom of God.[xii] However, neither did being in the Old covenant *prevent* Jewish people from coming into the Genesis 3:15/Abrahamic promise. This is Paul's point in Galatians 3:16–17—the promise of a spiritual kingdom was not "annulled" when the Mosaic covenant was made some 430 years later. That original "all the nations" promise to Abraham still stood.

The Promise in Hebrews 11

This analysis, that the Mosaic covenant itself did not give an eternal hope, is also consonant with Hebrews 11. Verse 1 tells us, "Now faith is the assurance of things hoped for, the conviction of things not seen," then the chapter lists many Old Testament people that had such faith.

The New Covenant

But nonetheless, the writer explains in v. 39, "though commended through their faith, [they] did not receive what was promised." What promise is it that all these Old Testament people believed in, but did not see? Let's look at the different people mentioned in relation to their place in the Bible story, none of whom had "received the promise," and see what we can learn.

Those who lived before the promise to Abraham:

Abel, Enoch, and Noah must have been looking back to a promise given earlier, and thus before Abraham was born—this can only be the Genesis 3:15 promise of the one who was to come and defeat Satan.

Those who lived after the promise to Abraham but before the Mosaic covenant:

Abraham, Sarah, Jacob, Joseph, and Isaac embraced the Abrahamic promise—which with a New Testament perspective we can see is, in effect, a restatement of the Genesis 3:15 promise.

Those under the Mosaic covenant but who did not live to see the promised land:

Moses made the covenant at Sinai with God but did not live to see the promised land.

Those who lived during the Mosaic era but not under its covenant:

Rahab.

Those who were under the Mosaic covenant and did live to see the promised land:

Gideon, Barak, Samson, Jephthah, David, and Samuel.

Many Christians today see the state of modern Israel is a fulfilment of Old Testament prophecy. But we can see from above that those that had experienced the earlier, earthly, promised land (for example, David) were not looking forward to another earthly one: "though commended through their faith, did not receive what was promised, since God had provided something better" (vv. 39–40). It is also clear that these Old Testament believers, both those that pre-dated and post-dated the Mosaic covenant, including the Gentile, Rahab, all looked forward to the same promise.

That promise—repeated to David (2 Samuel 7:12–17), and fulfilled in Christ—was the promise of a new heaven and a new earth in the presence of God. And it is that Genesis 3:15/Abrahamic spiritual promise that Jesus came to secure, to fulfil the hopes of those Old Testament believers, and offer to any Jew or Gentile, who would respond to his call, a place in that new heaven and earth.

But What of the Blood Line of Israel?

In Romans 9 Paul tackles what he knew would be the problem for his compatriots as he preached "his gospel" (Romans 2:16). That gospel, with its faith-based affinity union, clashed with the "flesh" (i.e., blood) union of the Mosaic covenant. He anticipates their question: "What now of this Israel 'of the flesh?'" He answers:

> to [the Israelites of the flesh] belong the adoption, the glory, the covenants, the giving of the law, the worship, and the promises. To them belong the patriarchs, and from their race, according to the flesh, is the Christ who is God over all, blessed forever. Amen. But it is not as though the word of God has failed. For not all who are descended from Israel belong to Israel, and not all are children of Abraham because they are his offspring, but "Through Isaac shall your offspring be named." (Romans 9:5–7)

Israel had many privileges under the Mosaic covenant, but automatic entry into the Abrahamic single seed promise was not one of them. In v. 8 Paul drives the point home:

> This means that it is *not* the *children of the flesh* [i.e. those of the Mosaic covenant blood line] who are the children of God, but it is those who are of the promise that are *counted as* offspring.

Paul is making the same point that he did in Galatians 3:11, "no one is justified before God by the [Mosaic] law." It is the same point that John makes in his Gospel (as above, John 1:12–13; 3:6)— to participate in the new covenant blessings Jewish people had, just like the

Gentiles, to come to the Bridegroom Messiah, and enter by faith in to the affinity union that he established with the church—a church that comprises all believers: past, present, and future. And then in vv. 25–26, Paul shows that what he is saying is rooted in their own Scriptures. He goes to the Hosea marital imagery:

> As indeed he says in Hosea, "Those who were not my people I will call 'my people' and her who was not beloved I will call 'beloved.'" And in the very place where it was said to them, "You are not my people," there they will be called "sons of the living God." (Romans 9:25–26)

With this new marriage, believing Gentiles are to be counted as being in the patriarch's family and thus included in God's promises alongside believing Jews, just as Hosea had prophesied.

THE NEW COVENANT DESTINATION IS A NEW CREATION

At the end of time the Bridegroom Messiah will come for the church that he has betrothed—it will include all those that have put their trust in God's promise recorded in Genesis 3:15, repeated to Abraham, and secured by the new covenant. The destination, it is clear, is not to a land to the east of the Mediterranean, but to "a better country" (Hebrews 11:16). Revelation tells us:

> Then I heard what seemed to be the voice of a great multitude, like the roar of many waters and like the sound of mighty peals of thunder, crying out, "Hallelujah! For the Lord our God the Almighty reigns. Let us rejoice and exult and give him the glory, for the marriage of the Lamb has come, and his Bride has made herself ready; it was granted her to clothe herself with fine linen, bright and pure"—for the fine linen is the righteous deeds of the saints. And the angel said to me, "Write this: Blessed are those who are invited to the marriage supper of the Lamb." And he said to me, "These are the true words of God." (Revelation 19:6–9)

> Then I saw a new heaven and a new earth, for the first heaven and the first earth had passed away, and the sea was no more. And I saw the holy city, new Jerusalem, coming down out of heaven from God, prepared as a bride adorned for her husband. And I heard a loud voice from the throne saying, "Behold, the dwelling place of God is with man. He will dwell with them, and they will be his people, and God himself will be with them as their God. He will wipe away every tear from their eyes, and death shall be no more, neither shall there be mourning, nor crying, nor pain anymore, for the former things have passed away." (Revelation 21:1–4)

IN SUMMARY

The new covenant swept all the old Mosaic covenant promises of a new and better future for Israel (a future that was to include the Gentiles) in to the new "marriage" of Christ and the church to be consummated at the end of time. In this new covenant: the new exodus promised (Hosea 1:11) is to be an exodus out of this world to the next (Hebrews 12:18–25); the promised new land is a new heavens and earth (2 Peter 3:13); the reunited nation (Jeremiah 31:1) is the one people of God, the church, comprising of all those who before Christ trusted in the Abrahamic promise (Hebrews 11), and subsequently, those who trusted in the Bridegroom Messiah who crystallised that promise in the new covenant (John 3:16; Ephesians 2:11–16); and the rebuilt temple (Ezekiel 40–44) is the church—Jesus's own body (John 2:19–21; 1 Corinthians 12:27).

Thus, we can see that the new covenant, although a marital covenant, just as the old covenant was, is in fact radically different. In that it is:

1   A covenant that is based on a different promise to that of the old covenant—the "all the nations" promise to Abraham in Genesis 22:17–18, not the one nation promise fulfilled in the Mosaic covenant.

2   A covenant whose bridal community (the church) is based on a Genesis 2:24 marital affinity union, not a union based on a Genesis 2:23 blood line.

The New Covenant

3   A covenant that, unlike the old covenant, actually justifies its members.

4   A covenant that has a different outcome—a spiritual kingdom, not an earthly kingdom.

5   A covenant that has a different "badge" of membership—circumcision of the heart evidenced in a life of faith. (Romans 2:28–29)

However, the old and new covenants did share a common purpose—to reveal the majesty, holiness, and mercy of God, and ultimately, bring about the salvation of his people. But the old covenant in its many types and shadows only *pointed* to that salvation—it was the new covenant that delivered it. The glory of the new covenant would be diminished without the old covenant, nonetheless the new covenant stands on its own. Because, as we shall see in the next chapter, Jesus's blood was sufficient to deliver God's people straight into the Abrahamic promise, and thus, at the end of time, in to a restored Eden—a new heavens and new earth.

CHAPTER FOUR

THE CROSS

Some would see that there are more than twenty reasons given in the New Testament as to why Jesus came.[xiii] Perhaps most would say that he came to die on the cross to pay for our sins. He certainly did do that, as we see in Colossians:

> And you, who were dead in your trespasses and the uncircumcision of your flesh, God made alive together with him, having forgiven us all our trespasses, by cancelling the record of debt that stood against us with its legal demands. This he set aside, nailing it to the cross. (Colossians 2:13–14)

Our Western mind-set is perhaps more comfortable with these legal and accountancy metaphors of "trespass" and "debt." They lend themselves to a Bible story that apparently portrays a rather clinical God looking to balance the books, to settle the accounts, to do justice. While not denying that the cross accomplished such, from the marital imagery perspective they were the means to an end, and not an end in themselves.

That marital imagery tells us that the goal of Jesus's incarnation and death was to inaugurate a new covenant, that is, to inaugurate a new *marriage*—and it is the marital imagery that is the heartbeat of the Bible's story from Genesis to Revelation. Thus Jesus came to offer a betrothal to both Jew and Gentile, to offer a restored relationship with God in a new heavens and earth. But to make that betrothal offer, as we shall see now, he had to shed his blood on the cross.

Three things were required for the Bridegroom Messiah to accomplish his mission: the bride price required of all Jewish bridegrooms had to be paid; the law of marriage that would have prevented any such remarriage had to be fulfilled; and the bride had to be cleansed of the stain of sin so she could be present herself as a virgin bride.

THE BRIDE PRICE

In Jewish culture before a marriage could be agreed by the two families involved, the prospective bridegroom would pay to the bride's father a sum of money, called in Hebrew the *mohar*. An example is in Exodus 22:17 (where ESV translates *mohar* as "bride price"). In some cases, the money would then be passed to the bride by her father for the couple to use in their life together. The West is more familiar with a dowry, where the bride's father gives her a sum of money on marriage. However, the giving of a *mohar* is still evidenced in many cultures today—including West Africa, Madagascar, and parts of eastern Europe. This explains this statement of Paul:

> Or do you not know that your body is a temple of the Holy Spirit within you, whom you have from God? You are not your own, for you were bought with a price. So glorify God in your body. (1 Corinthians 6:19–20)

It is Jesus, the divine bridegroom, who pays the *mohar* for his bride. Hosea, uniquely in the Old Testament marital imagery, speaks of this future betrothal for God's people:

> And I will betroth you to me forever. I will betroth you to me in righteousness and in justice, in steadfast love and in mercy. I will betroth you to me in faithfulness. And you shall know the LORD. (Hosea 2:19–20)

Then, in chapter 3, God speaks again through Hosea, whose wayward wife Gomer is a symbol of Israel, and tells us that the new marriage is to be preceded by a betrothal period—and it is a betrothal with a *mohar* ("fifteen shekels of silver and a homer and a lethech of barley"):

> And the LORD said to me, "Go again, love a woman who is loved by another man and is an adulteress, even as the LORD loves the children of Israel, though they turn to other gods and love cakes of raisins." So I bought her for fifteen shekels of silver and a homer and a lethech of barley. And I said to her, "You must dwell as mine for many days. You shall not play the whore, or belong to another man; so will I also be to you." For the children of Israel shall dwell many days without king

or prince, without sacrifice or pillar, without ephod or household gods. Afterwards the children of Israel shall return and seek the LORD their God, and David their king, and they shall come in fear to the LORD and to his goodness in the latter days. (Hosea 3)

A virgin can certainly expect a *mohar*, but it would be unusual to give one for a woman of low repute such as Gomer. During this betrothal time (Hosea's prophecy calls it the "latter days") many Jewish people will turn in faith to "David their king" (Hosea 3:5)—that is, the Lord Jesus Christ. Paul's comment in 2 Corinthians 11:2 also refers to this time, "For I feel a divine jealousy for you, for I betrothed you to one husband, to present you as a pure virgin to Christ"—it was the responsibility of the bride's father, having received the *mohar*, to ensure his daughter remained a virgin as she awaited her bridegroom.

And so, Jesus goes to the cross to pay the price for his bride as prophesied. It was customary for Jewish bridegrooms to dress like a priest with a seamless robe and a crown on their wedding day (Exodus 28:31–32; cf. Isaiah 61:10; Song of Solomon 3:11)—just as Jesus wore on the day of his crucifixion (Matthew 27:27–29; John 19:23). This symbolism on the cross foreshadows the marriage supper of the Lamb at the end of time.

Paul, in his letter to Timothy, describes the situation as we await Jesus's return:

> Therefore I endure everything for the sake of the elect, that they also may obtain the salvation that is in Christ Jesus with eternal glory. The saying is trustworthy, for: If we have died with him, we will also live with him; if we endure, we will also reign with him; if we deny him, he also will deny us; if we are faithless, he remains faithful—for he cannot deny himself. (2 Timothy 2:10–13)

The bridegroom would be honour-bound to come for his bride having promised her father and paid the *mohar* to seal the arrangement—only her sexual unfaithfulness could justify him breaking that promise. Therefore, Joseph was described as a just man even though he sought to break their betrothal and "divorce" Mary because of her presumed sexual unfaithfulness (Matthew 1:18–19).

Paul is saying here in 2 Timothy that even if Christian believers give up hope that Jesus would ever come for them he would still honour his promise. Only if we "deny him," only if we walk away from him and choose another, will he deny us. Many Christians rightly hold to the view that true believers are secure with Christ, but those in the visible church that have a false profession will be lost, as Jesus explains in Matthew 7:21–23.

THE LAW OF MARRIAGE

The Double Lock

It will be remembered from chapter 1 that the Deuteronomy 24 law of marriage embraced a double lock. Firstly, although a wife could divorce her husband, she could not go on to marry anybody else without the certificate which he alone could issue. Secondly, even with the certificate, she could never remarry that first husband, even if the husband she was divorcing gave permission for that.

This double lock bound all humanity (including Israel) to Satan — we were all banished from God's presence when Adam was exiled ("divorced") from God. Galatians 3:22 can be translated either as "the Scripture imprisoned everything under sin" or, "the Scriptures declare that we are all [Jew and Gentile] prisoners of sin" — as Jesus himself explains to the Jews who questioned him:

> So Jesus said to the Jews who had believed in him, "If you abide in my word, you are truly my disciples, and you will know the truth, and the truth will set you free." They answered him, "We are offspring of Abraham and have never been enslaved to anyone. How is it that you say, 'You will become free'"? Jesus answered them, "Truly, truly, I say to you, everyone who commits sin is a slave to sin. The slave does not remain in the house forever; the son remains forever. So if the Son sets you free, you will be free indeed." (John 8:31–36)

The Bridegroom Messiah

Jesus is saying that their relationship with Abraham does not mean they are not also in a relationship with Sin. But it might be thought that God could not take Israel as a "wife" at Sinai if she, like the rest of humanity, was bound in a relationship to Satan. This only serves to emphasise that the Mosaic covenant was not a covenant to take people back into the presence of God. It was not a fulfilment of the Genesis 3:15 prophecy—neither Satan nor the seed of the woman was bruised. It was instead an earthly, temporary covenant that prefigured the remarriage with Christ at the eschaton. For *that* marriage (unlike Sinai) a death was required to release the elect from their relationship to Sin. Satan was untroubled by the Mosaic covenant—all mankind was still firmly in his grasp.

The emphasis in the marital imagery is on that relationship with Sin, rather than on actual sins committed. An illustration might help explain the difference between Sin as a spiritual entity, and the *sins* we commit because of our relationship with Sin. I recently stayed in a home where they had found a stain on a wall. Somewhat puzzled, they cleaned it off and redecorated—but some weeks later the stain reappeared. On further investigation they found that inside the wall there was an old waterpipe that had corroded and was leaking. It had to be cut out and the stain cleaned again. It has not come back since.

We know that Jesus died to pay for the sins we have committed, but those sins are only the symptom of our problem. We have seen that Paul tells us that, "Scripture has shut up everyone under sin" (Galatians 3:22 NASB). He is saying that the source of our problem is that all Adamic humanity, Jew and Gentile, are locked in a relationship (a "marriage") with Sin. God's people need to be taken out of that bridal community, and brought into Jesus's own bridal community—out of the "body of Sin" where we are enslaved to Sin (Romans 6:6), and into the "body of Christ" (Romans 7:4).

But how is this to be achieved? In addition to the law of marriage recorded in Deuteronomy 24, Scripture teaches that if a wife or husband dies, their relationship is terminated. Thus when asked about a woman who had had seven husbands, Jesus explains that, "in the resurrection they neither marry nor are given in marriage, but are like angels in heaven" (Matthew 22:30). Paul further clarifies this in 1

Corinthians 7:39: "A wife is bound to her husband as long as he lives. But if her husband dies, she is free to be married to whom she wishes, only in the Lord." This teaching—we might call it a "law"—brings us to the heart of the gospel and the Genesis 3:15 prophecy. That prophecy foresaw the death of Christ on the cross, a death that was necessary to release the elect of Adamic humanity from the hold of Satan.

The First Lock Released: No Longer Bound

It was pointed out in our first chapter that the theme of Romans 6 is that the Roman believers were previously bound to Sin but were released by Christ's death to enable them instead to serve Christ. We read there that:

> Now if we have died with Christ, we believe that we will also live with him ... So you also must consider yourselves dead to sin and alive to God in Christ Jesus ... But now that you have been set free from sin and have become slaves of God, the fruit you get leads to sanctification and its end, eternal life. (Romans 6:8, 11, 22)

Then chapter 7 opens with this statement:

> Or do you not know, brothers—for I am speaking to those who know the law—that the law is binding on a person only as long as he lives? For a married woman is bound by law to her husband while he lives, but if her husband dies she is released from the *law of marriage*. Accordingly, she will be called an adulteress if she lives with another man while her husband is alive. But if her husband dies, she is free from *that law*, and if she marries another man she is not an adulteress. Likewise, my brothers, you also have died to the law [of marriage] through the body of Christ, so *that you may belong to another*, to him who has been raised from the dead, in order that we may bear fruit for God. (Romans 7:1–4)

Paul is saying to the Romans, that as believers in Christ, Jesus's death is counted as *their* death, and thus they have been released from their relationship with Sin. They can now "belong to another" (v. 4—KJV has "be married to another"). The first of the double locks has been legitimately released. No law has been broken. No law has been cancelled. And yet believers are no longer bound to Sin. In other words, they are free to marry another *without* the certificate from their "husband." Satan's power over them is broken. We might say that believers have been released "according to" or "by means of the law"—the law that death terminates a marriage.

This understanding perhaps explains Paul's comment in Galatians 2:19, a comment that has puzzled many Bible students, "For through the law [that is, according to/by means of the law] I [Paul] died to the law [of marriage], so that I might live to God." It seems that Paul is saying precisely the same here as in Roman 7:4—no law has been broken, rather he has been released from the law of marriage by means of the law of marriage. His "death in Christ" meant that *that* law no longer applied. Many believe that Paul in Galatians 2:19 and Romans 7:4 (despite specifically referring to the law of marriage in the latter) is talking about the Mosaic law. In Some Reflections at the end of the book I give further consideration to that more traditional interpretation.

The Second Lock Released: A Virgin Bride

But what about the second aspect of the law of marriage "double lock" that forbids a wife to ever remarry her first husband? A prophecy of Jeremiah foresaw this situation, and in light of New Testament teaching we can now see that Christ's blood shed on the cross washed clean all those that would believe (1 John 1:7; Revelation 7:13–14). They are now deemed a virgin bride—the past has been wiped away:

> "At that time, declares the LORD, I will be the God of all the clans of Israel, and they shall be my people." Thus says the LORD: "The people who survived the sword found grace in the wilderness; when Israel sought for rest, the LORD appeared to him from far away. I have loved you with an everlasting love; therefore I have continued my faithfulness to you. Again I will build you, and you shall be built, O virgin Israel! Again you shall adorn yourself with tambourines and shall go forth in the dance of the merrymakers." (Jeremiah 31:1–4)

A virgin is not necessarily a bride. If the purpose of Jesus's death was solely to cleanse his people from their sins this would *not* bring them into God's presence. Instead, Jesus came to betroth his people, and to that end he had to cleanse his bride to give all those in the church a new start in their relationship with God. The sins committed when we were in the old marriage to Sin are wiped away. What is more, this bride can now be the bride of a High Priest, as Jesus is described — such could only marry a virgin (Leviticus 21:13; Hebrews 9:11).

THE BRIDEGROOM MESSIAH IS A MAN

To grasp something of the significance of what Jesus endured on the cross so as to betroth his bride, we need to understand that Christ was both fully God and fully man — this dual nature is what theologians call the "hypostatic union." There is a rightful emphasis in the Christian church on Jesus's deity, but there is perhaps a danger that such overshadows his very real humanity. Jesus had a human mother but no human father (Luke 1:26–38; Galatians 4:4), he was revealed in human form (Philippians 2:7–8; Romans 8:3) — it was a body that could be touched (1 John 1:1–3). Although he became what he was not (a man), he remained what he was, God (John 1:1–3, 14). And yet, as we see from the accounts of his life in the Gospels, his two natures were kept separate, and only rarely is his deity displayed. But when the soldiers and Pharisees came to arrest Jesus in the garden of Gethsemane, John gives this account:

> "Whom do you seek?" They answered him, "Jesus of Nazareth." Jesus said to them, "I am he." Judas, who betrayed him, was standing with them. When Jesus said to them, "I am he," they drew back and fell to the ground. (John 18:4–6)

When Moses at the burning bush asked for God's name, he said, "I am who I am" (Exodus 3:14). It seems from the reaction in Gethsemane that Jesus chose that moment to identify himself, at least momentarily, as God in the flesh.

But it is his "humanness" that is to the fore in the Gospels. He had half brothers and sisters, walked in the fields of Nazareth, attended the synagogue, was tired, thirsty, and wept over Lazarus's death. He had

The Bridegroom Messiah

a personality, thoughts, and emotions. And what is more, he remained a man in bodily form after his resurrection. And we know that we also, in the new heavens and new earth, will have a body that will be 'like his glorious body' (Philippians 3:21).

It was as a man that Jesus steadfastly set his face to go to Jerusalem (Luke 9:51). When he was arrested in Gethsemane it is clear, even then, that he could have chosen not to go through with it:

> "Do you think that I cannot appeal to my Father, and he will at once send me more than twelve legions of angels? But how then should the Scriptures be fulfilled, that it must be so?" (Matthew 26:53–54)

He knew there was no other way to wrestle the elect from Satan's hold except by means of his incarnation and subsequent death on the cross:

> "Now is my soul troubled. And what shall I say? 'Father, save me from this hour'? But for this purpose I have come to this hour." (John 12:27)

And thus it was as a man that he contemplated the full horror of what awaited him:

> And going a little farther he fell on his face and prayed, saying, "My Father, if it be possible, let this cup pass from me; nevertheless, not as I will, but as you will." (Matthew 26:39)

He knew his death was going to be different from ours, for he was to bear the weight of our sin (1 Peter 2:24). He sought the comfort and companionship of his disciples, but just at the time he needed them most, they let him down:

> And he came to the disciples and found them sleeping. And he said to Peter, "So, could you not watch with me one hour?" (Matthew 26:40)

But perhaps most mysteriously of all when we contemplate Jesus's dual nature, when addressing the Ephesian elders, Paul said:

> "Pay careful attention to yourselves and to all the flock, in which the Holy Spirit has made you overseers, to care for the church of God, which he obtained with his own blood." (Acts 20:28)

The church was bought with the blood of a *man*—but that man was God in the flesh. The central purpose of the cross was not about Jesus "paying the price" in his blood for the various laws that mankind had broken. Those broken laws were a symptom of a broken relationship. Jesus shed his blood as the Bridegroom Messiah to offer all who would come a place by his side at the marriage supper of the Lamb.

THE NEW COVENANT CONSUMMATED

The focus of the Book of Revelation is on the consummation of the long-promised marriage of God and his people that is the Bible's overarching story. The very title "Revelation," derived from its first verse, "The revelation of Jesus Christ" is probably a reflection of the ancient Jewish custom of the bridegroom lifting the veil covering his bride's face. And it is at the climax of the book that we are told that the "marriage of the Lamb has come, and his bride has made herself ready" (Revelation 19:7). The bridegroom has come to collect his bride in the tradition of Jewish weddings. The bride is the church, the elect, that is any who turn by faith to Christ. The bride consists of both Jews and Gentiles—all who had been bound to Sin are now invited to the wedding supper of the Lamb where Jesus will take the church, his own body, to himself, and thus restore the Edenic bliss of Adam and Eve.

But this new Eden is different. At the cross Jesus, "disarmed the powers and authorities, he made a public spectacle of them, triumphing over them by the cross." (Colossians 2:15 NIV). The devil is destroyed:

> Since therefore the children share in flesh and blood, he himself likewise partook of the same things, that through death he might destroy the one who has the power of death, that is, the devil. (Hebrews 2:14)

The Bridegroom Messiah

Satan will never again trouble God's people. We have gained more than we lost. We will be secure in God's presence forevermore because of what Jesus, our Bridegroom Messiah, achieved for us on the cross. He came to fulfil God's promise given at the very gates of Eden and recorded for us in Genesis 3:15. He came to free us from Satan's grasp and bring us back into the very presence of God. To do that he had to die fulfil God's own marriage law—his death became our death, and his shed blood cleansed our sins. The double lock was broken. His bride was made ready for the wedding supper of the Lamb. We will then surely sing:

> I stand amazed in the presence, Of Jesus the Nazarene
> And I wonder how He could love me, A sinner condemned, unclean.
>
> *How marvellous, how wonderful, And my song shall ever be.*
> *How marvellous, how wonderful, Is my Saviour's love for me.*
>
> For me it was in the garden, He prayed, "Not my will, but thine"
> He had no tears for His own griefs, But sweat drops of blood for mine.
>
> He took my sins and my sorrows, He made them His very own;
> He bore the burden to Calv'ry, And suffered and died alone.
>
> When with the ransomed in glory, His face I at last shall see,
> 'Twill be my joy thro' the ages, To sing of His love for me.[xiv]

SOME REFLECTIONS

Some of the issues raised in the main body of the book are considered further here, with reading suggestions for those that want to explore them more deeply.

THE CROSS AND THE MOSAIC COVENANT

Many (most?) believe that when Jesus died, he died to free humanity from the onerous Mosaic covenant. Such, at times, seems to be Paul's own perspective. When addressing the Roman believers, he tells them that they had "died to the law" (Romans 7:4). But we will see below that there are many problems with this understanding.

The Gentiles in the Church at Rome Were Not Part of The Mosaic Covenant

Why would Paul in his letter to the Romans, the most detailed exposition of the gospel in the New Testament, focus on the need for the believers there to be released from the Mosaic law? Not only are there many Greek names in the salutations of the last chapter, Paul's comment in the opening chapter suggests it was predominantly a Gentile church:

> I want you to know, brothers, that I have often intended to come to you (but thus far have been prevented), in order that I may reap some harvest among you as well as among the rest of the Gentiles. (Romans 1:13)

The Gentiles had no part in the Mosaic covenant (a point N.T. Wright makes[1])— they were specifically excluded from it as Deuteronomy 7:6 makes clear (but see comments below regarding the Westminster Confession). Furthermore, Paul makes the point in both Romans 2:10–14, and in 1 Corinthians 9:20–21, that the Gentiles are "without the law"—and from the context of both it is clear he means the Mosaic law. It would seem to contradict the concept of a just God to hold them responsible for keeping the law codes of the Mosaic covenant, a covenant that they were not part of, and most knew little or nothing

---

[1] N.T. Wright, *The Climax of the Covenant* (Edinburgh: T & T Clark, 1991), 173.

about. So it should not be a surprise to find that nowhere does the New Testament teach this. Paul says that the Gentiles are to be held to account, not for the Mosaic laws, but for their failure to obey universal moral laws, examples of which he gives in Romans 1 (vv. 18–32), where he says:

> For what *can* be known about God [and his universal moral laws] is plain to [the Gentiles], because God has shown it to them. For his invisible attributes, namely, his eternal power and divine nature, have been clearly perceived, ever since the creation of the world, in the things that have been made. So they are without excuse. (Romans 1:19–20)

The Mosaic Covenant was Conditional

While the Mosaic covenant conditions were imposed, the covenant itself was not—Dennis McCarthy comments that, "the people are asked, never compelled, to enter into the relationship."[2] All subsequent generations after Sinai had a clear choice about it (see for example, Joshua 24, where Joshua pleads with Israel to remain in the covenant relationship with God). So why would a death be needed to extract anybody (Jew or Gentile) out of it?

Both Israel and Judah were Divorced from the Mosaic Covenant

The marital imagery of the Bible is consistent and clear. As we saw in chapter 1, Israel had already been freed from their covenant, not by a death, but by a "divorce" (the Assyrian exile in 722 BCE). And soon to follow was Judah (and Benjamin)—a divorce forewarned in Malachi 4, declared in Matthew 23, and enacted in the destruction of Jerusalem in 70 CE. God divorced both Israel and Judah. So why would a death be needed as well?[3]

---

[2] Dennis J. McCarthy, *Old Testament Covenant: A Survey of Current Opinions* (Stuttgart: Verlag Katholisches Biblewerk, 1967; Repr. Oxford: Blackwell, 1972), 46–48, 55.

[3] For a more comprehensive treatment of the Bible's marital imagery on this, and various other issues raised in the book, see: Colin Hamer, *Marital Imagery in the Bible: An Exploration of Genesis 2:24 and its Significance for the Understanding of New Testament Divorce and Remarriage Teaching* (London: Apostolos, 2015)

Some Reflections

The Cross was to Release the Elect from Sin—not the Mosaic Covenant

The problem for all humanity (Jew and Gentile) was that they were bound, not to the Mosaic covenant, but to Sin (John 8:31–38; Galatians 3:22). John 3:16 tells us that Jesus loved the "world" and gave himself that "all" might be saved—not just Jewish people.

The Cross was to Restore a Relationship

The central purpose of the cross was to take the elect out of their relationship with Sin and directly in to the Abrahamic promise—not to extract either Jew or Gentile out of the Mosaic covenant. The problem for both Jew and Gentile is the same, and it is not that old Mosaic covenant. All Adamic humanity are sinners, excluded from Eden, and locked in a relationship with the one who caused our exile—Satan. The cross was to address what at root is a relational problem—to rescue humanity from their relationship with Sin and restore their relationship to God. We can clearly see this relational aspect of God's character in his dealings with Israel. They were not "divorced" because they had not kept the more than 600 Pentateuchal laws— the sacrificial system was designed to keep them in fellowship with God even when they fell short of that ideal. They were divorced because they had forsaken him and persistently gone with other "gods."

Thus the central purpose of Jesus's mission was not about paying the price for the Mosaic laws that Israel had broken—nor for the laws of nature that the Gentiles had breached. The broken laws were a symptom of a broken relationship. The heart of the gospel is that Jesus came in fulfilment of the Genesis 3:15 prophecy to restore a relationship with God, not just for Israel, but to all who would come to him—the cross was to enable that to happen. The "law" that kept humanity out of Eden (Lewis's Deep Magic), and that had locked them in a relationship with Satan, had, in one way or another, to be fulfilled.

SOME OBJECTIONS CONSIDERED

Galatians 3

Some see that Paul tells believers in his letter to the Galatians that they needed to be released from the curse of the "Book of the Law"—that is, the Mosaic covenant:

> For all who rely on works of the law are under a curse; for it is written, "Cursed be everyone who does not abide by all things written in the Book of the Law, and do them." Now it is evident that no one is justified before God by the law, for "The righteous shall live by faith." But the law is not of faith, rather "The one who does them shall live by them." Christ redeemed us from the curse of the law by becoming a curse for us—for it is written, "Cursed is everyone who is hanged on a tree" —so that in Christ Jesus the blessing of Abraham might come to the Gentiles, so that we might receive the promised Spirit through faith. (Galatians 3:10–14)

If we look carefully, and consider the context, we can see that "the curse" is not at all in the "Book of the Law"—those "under the curse" are "those who rely on works of the law." Who are these people? They are not the Gentiles—the great proportion of humanity at that time (and today) knew little about any such book. Paul is talking about Jewish people, and Gentile converts in the Galatian church, who had been persuaded that keeping the Mosaic law was a necessary part of the Christian life.

As more study is done into New Testament times it is realised that many Jewish people, like Paul, "rejoiced in the law" ("as to righteousness under the law, blameless," Philippians 3:6)—it was their "badge" that they, and *not* the Gentiles, belonged to God. It was, it seems, only after Paul's conversion that he saw the danger of this understanding. Hence his statement in Galatians 3:10, "For all who rely on works of the law are under a curse."[4]

---

[4] See discussion in: Tom Holland, *Contours of Pauline Theology* (Fearn: Christian Focus, 2004), 210–12.

Some Reflections

Many in Israel thought that if they were circumcised, and attended the required ceremonies and feasts, their relationship with God was alright. It is a "legalism" that is a feature of many religions. Thus many in the visible church today think baptism and church attendance please God and secure their position in heaven. But Jesus warns that many professing Christians will be disappointed on the judgement day (Matthew 7:21–23).

Accordingly, the "curse of the law" is for those that think that keeping "all things written in the Book of the Law" can give them a relationship with God. Paul teaches the Galatians, a church that was troubled by those that said that keeping those Jewish laws was important, that Christ's death on the cross has paid the price to enable any, Jew or Gentile, to go straight into the Abrahamic blessing—the "Book of the Law" had been completely by-passed. For Israel, their marriage covenant had been made obsolete.

Ephesians 2

> For he himself is our peace, who has made us both one and has broken down in his flesh the dividing wall of hostility by abolishing the law of commandments expressed in ordinances, that he might create in himself one new man in place of the two, so making peace, and might reconcile us both to God in one body through the cross, thereby killing the hostility. (Ephesians 2:14–16)

The "law of commandments expressed in ordinances" is certainly a reference to the many Mosaic law codes. But how was it *abolished*? Hebrews tells that Jesus's death opened the "new and living way" of the new covenant that has made that old way obsolete: "we have confidence to enter the holy places by the blood of Jesus, by the new and living way that he opened for us through the curtain, that is, through his [torn] flesh" (Hebrews 10:19–20). It is a way open to Jew and Gentile.

Romans 7

Another New Testament passage which has led people to think that Jesus's death was primarily to satisfy the demands of the Mosaic code

The Bridegroom Messiah

is found in Paul's letter to the Romans. Tom Holland is an evangelical scholar with an international reputation and has spent some 40 years studying that letter. He claims that fundamental to Paul's argument is the concept that Jesus is the *Bridegroom Messiah*—and that it is impossible to understand what Paul is saying unless that is the frame of reference used.

In Romans 7, Paul brings his argument to a climax, preparing the way for his great declaration in Romans 8:1, "There is therefore now no condemnation for those who are in Christ Jesus." To do that he opens chapter 7 with a crucial marital illustration. However, because the "key" to unlocking Romans, as suggested by Holland (that is, the marital imagery), has been lost to the church, many struggle with Paul's illustration (many others simply ignore the problems it raises). Two scholars comment: C. H. Dodd says, "What, then, is the application of the illustration, or metaphor, or allegory, or whatever it is?"; and Joyce Little of the same passage, "the suggestion cannot be avoided that the analogy has somehow failed."[5]

Paul begins his argument in Romans 5 by explaining that death came from Adam (that is, that Adam took us all into a relationship that caused us to die) and life comes from Christ (that is, that Jesus takes the elect into a relationship that gives life). Thus he frames his explanation of the gospel between those two events—that is, the relationship with Sin that Adam took humanity into, and the new "marriage" enabled by the cross—the argument is *not* framed between the Mosaic Covenant and the cross. And in chapter 6 Paul drives this point home—the whole chapter is about the problem (our relationship with Sin) and its solution (the cross).

We cannot do justice here to all Paul's argument, instead we will look briefly at the opening verses of chapter 7, verses that have caused such difficulty to so many Bible scholars. The reader can find a full exegesis of Romans 7 that is in accord with the Bible's marital imagery, and

---

[5] J. A. Little, "Paul's Use of Analogy: A Structural Analysis of Romans 7:1–6," CBQ 46 (1984), 84–85; C. H. Dodd, The Epistle to the Romans (New York: Harper, 1932), 101.

Some Reflections

indeed the whole of Romans, in Tom Holland's *The Hope of the Nations*.[6]

Romans 7:1–13

The emphasis is added and my commentary is in square brackets:

[1] Or do you not know, brothers—for I am speaking to those who know the law—that the law is binding on a person only as long as he lives?

[2] For a married woman is bound *by* law to her husband while he lives, but if her husband dies she is *released* from the *law of marriage*. [N.T. Wright makes the crucial point that we are bound *by* the law, not that we are bound *to* the law, and argues, consonant with the Bible's marital imagery, that Paul is talking about the law of marriage.[7] The only marriage law in the Bible that binds anybody is Deuteronomy 24. That law precisely reflects the "law" that neither Adam or Israel could ever go back to God. Thus key to the exegesis of Romans 7, is to identify to whom, or to what, is Adamic humanity bound *by* that law of marriage. It is the central issue of man's dilemma, and of the gospel, and thus of Paul's argument.]

[3] Accordingly, she will be called an adulteress if she lives with another man while her husband is alive. But if her husband dies, she is free from that law, and if she marries another man she is not an adulteress. [A husband's death was the only way out of a marriage and into another marriage for a wife if her husband refused the certificate.]

[4] Likewise, my brothers, you also have died to the law [i.e. the Deuteronomy 24 law of marriage—the law (Lewis's Deep Magic) that bound Adamic humanity to their "husband," Sin] through the body of Christ [once either partner in the marriage dies the marriage is over, the point made in vv. 1–2. Thus when the elect "die in Christ"

---

[6] Tom Holland, *Hope for the Nations: Paul's Letter to the Romans* (London: Apostolos, 2015)

[7] N. T. Wright, 'The Letter to the Romans,' in The New Interpreter's Bible (Vol. X) Acts Introduction to Epistolary Literature Romans 1 Corinthians, ed. Leander E. Keck (Nashville, TN: Abingdon, 2002), 539, 559; see analysis of Wright's position in: Hamer, *Marital Imagery*, §9.4.2

The Bridegroom Messiah

(Romans 6:8) they are freed from their "marriage" to Sin], so that they might *belong to another* [KJV has "married to another"] to him [Jesus Christ] who has been raised from the dead, in order that we might bear fruit for God. [The more traditional understanding that Paul is talking about the Mosaic covenant collapses at this point, as some Bible exegetes point out. Neither Jew nor Gentile were ever "married to" or "belonged to" that Mosaic covenant—Israel was "married" to God, not the covenant, which they saw as their "wedding ring."]

[5] For while we were living in the flesh [that is, in Sin's family], our sinful passions, aroused by the law [the Edenic law Adam was given, as Paul explains in the very next verses 7–13], were [past tense] at work in our members [i.e. previously unconverted Jewish and Gentile church members] to bear fruit for death.

[6] But now we [Jew and Gentile] are *released from the law* [the Deuteronomy 24/Deep Magic law], having died [in Christ, Romans 6:8] to that which *held us captive*, so that we serve in the new way of the Spirit and not [serve] in the old way of the written [Mosaic] code. [The law of marriage bound "us" (Jew and Gentile) to Sin, who therefore held us all captive. It should be noted that the Mosaic covenant never held Jew or Gentile "captive," and certainly not to *itself*—it was the means by which the Jew served God, as Paul makes clear. It was the ontological law of marriage reflected in Deuteronomy 24 that held humanity captive to Satan. But previously the Mosaic "written code" was the only perceived way to please God for both Jews and Gentile proselytes. So Paul says, Christ's death—which has become our death—means that we can all (Jew and Gentile) now serve God, as he says, in a "new way"—a "new and living way" as Hebrews 10:19–20 describes it.]

[7] What then shall we say? That the law is sin? By no means! Yet if it had not been for the law, I would not have known sin. [Paul, having set the scene regarding the ontological law of marriage, now makes it clear what he sees is the reason for Christ's death—it is not to release mankind from the Mosaic covenant—it is to release mankind from their relationship with Sin. Thus he speaks next as if he were Adam,

Some Reflections

Lewis's Edmund in the allegory.[8] For I [that is, Adam] would not have known what it is to covet if the law had not said, "You shall not covet." [Adam coveted the fruit of the tree, Edmund coveted the Witch's Turkish Delight.]

[8] But sin [Satan], seizing an opportunity through the commandment, produced in me all kinds of covetousness. For apart from the law, sin [Satan] lies dead.

[9] I was once alive apart from the law [this is certainly Adam, not Paul, who had always lived under the law], but when the commandment came ["do not touch that tree"], sin [Satan] came alive and I died.

[10] The very commandment that promised [eternal] life proved to be death to me [unlike the Mosaic covenant which only offered a long *earthly* life, Deuteronomy 11:9; cf. Galatians 3:21].

[11] For sin [Satan], seizing an opportunity through the commandment, deceived me and through it killed me.

[12] So the law is holy, and the commandment is holy and righteous and good.

[13] Did that which is good [God's commandment to Adam], then, bring death to me? [Paul again anticipates the objection to his argument.] By no means! It was sin [Satan], producing death in me through what is good [God's law], in order that sin might be shown to be sin, and through the commandment might become sinful beyond measure.

This analysis is strengthened when Romans 7:24–25a is considered: "Wretched man that I am! Who will deliver me from this body of death? Thanks be to God through Jesus Christ our Lord!" Thus we are freed by Christ's death, not from the Mosaic covenant, but from the "body of death." The "body of death" is another name for the "body of Sin," which is elsewhere referred to as the "old man" (Romans

---

[8] Thiselton points out that most Pauline scholars accept that Paul in vv. 7–13 is not speaking autobiographically, "and some ascribe the identity of 'I' to Adam by implication": Thiselton, *The Hermeneutics of Doctrine*, 288.

6:6)—that is, unredeemed humanity, the precise opposite of Paul's "new man" (Ephesians 2:15)—the body of Christ.

In summary, we need to ask what "law" required a death (vv. 4, 6) before "you/we" (i.e. Paul and the believers in the church at Rome, Jew *and* Gentile) could be "released" from its requirements? He cannot mean the Mosaic law—Paul's Gentile readers were never subject to it. Nor can it be the law of Christ (that is, New Testament teaching, 1 Corinthians 9:21; Galatians 6:2), or universal moral law (Romans 1:18–32), as they still apply today. The law Paul is referring to is surely Lewis's Deep Magic of the "Emperor Beyond the Sea" referenced in chapter 1 of this book. Because Adam had succumbed to temptation he (and all humanity) was locked into a relationship with Sin.

It is this spiritual law that is the basis of Paul's argument in Romans 7—it is a law illustrated in the Deuteronomy 24 marriage teaching. And we have noted that that law, the Deep Magic, was not abolished—it was fulfilled by Jesus on the cross.

In contrast, Israel was free to walk away at any time from the temporary, temporal, volitional, conditional, Mosaic covenant. And it never held the Gentiles "captive" because they were never party to that covenant. Paul explains that the Mosaic covenant was "added for transgressions" and came 430 years after the Abrahamic promise that could give life, and that the Mosaic covenant "did not annul" that original promise (Galatians 3:15–21). Thus, access to God was still possible throughout the Mosaic period by means of that promise. And this is demonstrated in that many Old Testament believers did indeed believe in that promise as Hebrews 11 points out—making it clear that Israel was *not* held captive by the Mosaic covenant. But to crystallise that Abrahamic promise, to inaugurate the new covenant, a death was required, as Hebrews 10:19–20 explains.

Consequently, the New Covenant crystallises that original Abrahamic promise—it did not modify, or renew, the Mosaic covenant, which was now "obsolete" (Hebrews 8:13). And to make that fact clear, the Mosaic covenant was finally terminated, as we have seen, by a divorce (not a death) in 70 CE (i.e. more than 30 years after Jesus's death).

Some Reflections

National Israel

A possible objection to the analysis of the New Covenant in light of its marital imagery—an imagery which teaches that God has terminated his relationship with national Israel with two divorces—is that God promised Abraham the land "forever" (Genesis 13:15). It is argued that it is only to be expected that God would honour that promise, and therefore one day, national Israel will occupy their land again. But the Mosaic covenant that crystallised this aspect of the Abrahamic promise was conditional. For example, Exodus 19:5, "Now therefore, if you will indeed obey my voice and keep my covenant, you shall be my treasured possession among all peoples, for all the earth is mine"—and Israel manifestly and repeatedly failed to keep their side of the covenant (as we saw in chapter 1). Dennis McCarthy was one of the leading scholars of the 20th century on biblical covenants, and he saw the Mosaic covenant was both volitional and conditional, and that "the attempt" by theologians to see it as the same "covenant form" as other biblical covenants "has failed."[9]

In contrast, the new covenant that crystallised the spiritual aspect of the promise is for a new heavens and new earth—and although entrance is conditional on faith, it is God himself who gives us that faith to secure both our entrance in to his presence, and our eternal future there (Ephesians 2:8). And Hebrews 11 makes it clear that those under the Mosaic covenant, who despite experiencing the original (earthly) promised land, had not received "what was promised" (Hebrews 11:38).

THE PLACE OF THE MOSAIC LAW TODAY

It has been argued that the marital imagery demonstrates that the new covenant is different to the Mosaic covenant—and that the Gentiles had never had a part in that old covenant. Thus the question arises: "What place does that Mosaic covenant's laws have in the life of a Christian believer today—Jew or Gentile?" Some would point to this statement by Jesus:

---

[9] McCarthy, *Old Testament Covenant*, 46–58.

The Bridegroom Messiah

> Do not think that I have come to abolish the Law or the Prophets; I have not come to abolish them but to fulfil them. For truly, I say to you, until heaven and earth pass away, not an iota, not a dot, will pass from the Law until all is accomplished. (Matthew 5:17–18)

But if taken at face value, Jesus's words would seem to contradict other clear New Testament teaching. For example:

> So then, the law was our guardian until Christ came, in order that we might be justified by faith. But now that faith has come, we are no longer under a guardian, for in Christ Jesus you are all sons of God, through faith. (Galatians 3:24–26)

And Ephesians 2:15 states, "by abolishing the law of commandments expressed in ordinances, that he might create in himself one new man in place of the two, so making peace."

In light of such teaching, no Christian thinks that all the many Pentateuchal laws apply today. So it seems that in Matthew 5 Jesus is saying that he *fulfilled* the law's many types and shadows. And having fulfilled them, the purpose of that Mosaic covenant had come to an end. However, this matter is extensively debated by Christians today and it is beyond the scope of this little book to do justice to the protagonists of all the different views. But, in brief, there are three perspectives.

The 1646 Westminster Confession Perspective

The Westminster Confession position is rooted in Reformed teaching as expressed by John Calvin and is influential in churches worldwide—in particular, in Presbyterian churches. As we saw in chapter 1, Calvin believed, with other Reformers, in the essential unity of the old and new covenants. They saw that the "substance" of the two covenants was the same, even though the "circumstance" (national Israel versus the gospel era) was different. O. Palmer Robertson in his book *The Christ of the Covenants,* published by the Presbyterian and Reformed company, sees that when Deuteronomy 5:2 says, "The LORD our God made a covenant with us in Horeb," that the "us" includes all subsequent generations of believers—Jew or

Gentile.[10] This understanding facilitates the perception that the old and new covenants have a continuity, which in turn supports the concepts of paedobaptism and a national church linked to the state.

The 1689 London Baptist Confession Perspective

Pascal Denault points out that the 17th century Particular Baptists had a different perspective to that of the Westminster Confession. They saw that the Mosaic covenant was, in contrast to the new covenant, conditional, temporal, and temporary. The 1689 London Baptist Confession reflected that different understanding.[11]

However, common to those that hold to both the Westminster and the 1689 confessions, is the view that the Mosaic covenant law codes were of three different kinds: moral, civil, and ceremonial. And while Jesus fulfilled the types and shadows of the ceremonial law, and the civil laws of Israel clearly cannot be universally applied in the gospel era — all the moral teaching of that covenant is thought to come through to the New Testament era. This view is expressed in a PhD study by Philip Ross, *From the Finger of God*, published in 2010.[12]

The New Covenant Theology Perspective

A third perspective is that of New Covenant Theology (NCT). Believers of this persuasion see that the Mosaic covenant in its entirety is replaced by the new covenant. They agree with the confessional positions (as above) that the Mosaic covenant, in all its aspects, reveals the mind of God, and thus all of it is profitable (as 2 Timothy 3:16–17 affirms) — not least in the way it foreshadows the work of Christ. And that without such, the New Testament cannot be properly understood. NCT people further agree that God's moral law is binding, but not because it is in the Mosaic covenant — but because it

---

[10] Palmer O. Robertson, *The Christ of the Covenants* (Phillipsburg, NJ: Presbyterian and Reformed, 1980), 35–37.

[11] Pascal Denault, *The Distinctiveness of Baptist Covenant Theology: A Comparison between Seventeenth Century Particular Baptist and Paedobaptist Federalism* (Birmingham, AL: Solid Ground Christian Books, 2013). For a tabulated comparison of the Westminster and the 1689 confessions see: http://www.proginosko.com/docs/wcf_sdfo_lbcf.html

[12] Philip S. Ross, *From the Finger of God: The Biblical and Theological Basis for the Threefold Division of the Law* (Fearn: Christian Focus, 2010)

The Bridegroom Messiah

is God's moral law. And while principles can be argued from the Mosaic covenant, they see that Christians can only be bound by what is articulated in the Old Testament as applying to all people—and all that the New Testament teaches. The latter is described as the "law of Christ" (1 Corinthians 9:21; Galatians 6:2), and includes expressions of God's moral law as listed in Romans 1.

Jason Meyer's PhD, published as *The End of the Law*, articulates what would probably be described as an NCT view, in that he sees that the whole Mosaic covenant was replaced by the new covenant.[13] Consonant with the marital imagery (although he does not make that point), Meyer takes a relational view of Paul's understanding of the "old man" (Romans 6:6 KJV)—which Meyer takes to be Adamic humanity—and the "new man," the church (Ephesians 2:15). He thus sees that one reason Jesus came was to take the elect *out* of one relationship, "in Adam," *in* to another relationship, 'in Christ' via the Abrahamic promise.[14]

The Marital Imagery Perspective

The marital imagery perspective does not appear to be consonant with the Westminster Confession understanding of a unity between the Mosaic and new covenants. In chapter 1 the differences between Genesis 2:23 and Genesis 2:24 were pointed out. The former describes Eve's relationship with Adam—it is a blood relationship. Genesis 2:23 tells us that Eve came from Adam (she was his "bone and flesh")—just as Jacob came from Abraham, as did the whole of Israel—and such seems to have been their own perspective: "Then all the tribes of

---

[13] Jason C. Meyer, *The End of the Law: Mosaic Covenant in Pauline Theology* (Nashville, TN: B&H, 2009).

[14] Meyer, *The End of the Law*, 41–46. Meyer states: "The relational view asserts that the "old man" stands for who we were in Adam ... the cross put an end to our relational ties to Adam." I would suggest that the New Testament does not teach that Christ came to take the elect out of their relationship with Adam. Rather, that humanity was taken by Adam into a relationship with Sin, and it is the relationship with Sin that is the problem. Thus Romans speaks of the "old man" as unredeemed Adamic humanity in the "body of sin" (the people in a relationship with Sin) as opposed to the "new man" (Ephesians 2:15)—believers who are in the "body of Christ" (those in a relationship with Christ). The marital imagery sees believers as being freed from the former to enter the latter. See: Hamer, *Marital Imagery*, §1.4.2; §1.4.3

Some Reflections

Israel came to David at Hebron and said, 'Behold, we are your bone and flesh'" (2 Samuel 5:1). Thus it can be said that Israel occupies the same conceptual domain as Genesis 2:23.

However, the affinity relationship of Genesis 2:24 is quite different—a wife is brought in to a new family by her own choice by means of a covenant. In Ephesians 5:31–32 Paul says that Genesis 2:24 represents Christ and the church and calls it a profound mystery.

Thus the different concepts contained in Genesis 2:23 and Genesis 2:24 reflect the old and new covenants respectively. Scholars have puzzled about the placing of Genesis 2:24 in the Edenic story as it refers to a time after Adam's exile from the garden when such had not yet happened—some see it as an insertion by a later scribe. But perhaps the juxtaposition of those two verses was the divine intention? A foreshadowing of the drama of God's plan of salvation by means of two different covenants.

But throughout its history the church has believed that Genesis 2:24 refers to Adam and Eve—the two verses have been conflated in our minds. Consequently, the meaning of Paul's statement in Ephesians 5:31–32, where he explains the affinity basis of the new covenant, has also been lost. I suggest that if the Reformers had engaged with the New Testament marital imagery where the Bridegroom Messiah, the seed of Abraham, offers the church a betrothal based on a Genesis 2:24 affinity union, they might not have conflated the Mosaic and new covenants in the way they appear to have done. It was their understanding that was incorporated into the Westminster Confession.

Thus the marital imagery is closer to the separation of the covenants as outlined in the 1689 Confession. However, that confession sees a continuation of the Mosaic moral codes into the new covenant. But in the imagery, the "divorce" of Israel by God does appear to represent a clear break in God's relationship with that people group. That divorce was, as we have seen, no rhetorical device:

> I will cut off Israel from the land that I have given them, and the house that I have consecrated for my name I will cast out of my sight, and Israel will become a proverb and a byword

among all peoples. And this house will become a heap of ruins. Everyone passing by it will be astonished and will hiss, and they will say, "Why has the LORD done thus to this land and to this house?" (1 Kings 9:7–8)

As the function of the Mosaic covenant was to regulate God's relationship with Israel, it would appear to be difficult to argue that a selection of those laws, by virtue of them being in that old covenant, are now included in the new covenant, unless they are expressly said to do so. As Jason Meyer points out, neither the Old nor the New Testament make a threefold distinction in the law (moral, civil, ceremonial), and any division of such by a subsequent exegete has its problems.[15] Thus the marital imagery lends support to the "end of the [Mosaic] law" position of NCT.

---

[15] Meyer, *The End of the Law*, 282.

Some Reflections

Endnotes

[i] William J. Dumbrell, *Covenant and Creation: An Old Testament Covenant Theology* (Milton Keynes: Paternoster, 2013), 50–51, 129, 259.

[ii] See: Anthony C. Thiselton, *The Hermeneutics of Doctrine* (Grand Rapids: Eerdmans, 2007), 283–88.

[iii] Genesis 3:23 uses שׁלח ('to send' or 'to let go') where the context is, or appears to be, divorce in Genesis 21:14, Deuteronomy 21:14; 22:19, 29; 24:4, Jeremiah 3:1, 8, Malachi 2:16; similarly, Genesis 3:24 uses גרשׁ ('to cast out') which is employed in Genesis 21:10, Leviticus 21:7, 14; 22:13, Numbers 30:9, and Ezekiel 44:22.

[iv] Most Bible versions translate the Greek *doulos* in passages where it is used to describe our relationship to Satan (Romans 6:6), or to Christ (Romans 6:22), as "slave"—but some translate it as "servant." The relationship of unredeemed humanity to Satan is treated in Scripture as a marital covenant, as is the elect's relationship to Christ. The difference is that the marital covenant unredeemed humanity has with Satan is determined by the Deuteronomy 24 law of marriage—thus unredeemed humanity is not free to leave Satan to "serve" another. In that sense the "slave" translation has some merit, but I suggest it is less successful when applied to the relationship the believer has with Christ.

[v] For example, Seth D. Postell, *Adam as Israel: Genesis 1-3 as the Introduction to the Torah and Tanakh* (Eugene, OR: Pickwick, 2011).

[vi] Lewis C. S., *The Lion, the Witch and the Wardrobe* (New York: HarperCollins, 1950), 141–42.

[vii] Phillip J. Long, *Jesus the Bridegroom: The Origin of the Eschatological Feast as a Wedding Banquet in the Synoptic Gospels* (Eugene, OR: Pickwick, 2013),194.

[viii] Klyne Snodgrass sees that the three parables are warnings to Israel of a coming judgement: Klyne R. Snodgrass, "Reading and Overreading the Parables in Jesus the Victory of God," in *Jesus and the Restoration of Israel* (ed. Carey C. Newman; Downers Grove, IL: InterVarsity, 1999), 66–67.

[ix] Collins, Jack. "A Syntactical Note (Genesis 3:15): Is the Woman's Seed Singular or Plural," *Tyndale Bulletin* 48.1 (1997): 139–48; Alexander, Desmond T. "Further Observations on the Term 'Seed' in Genesis," *Tyndale Bulletin* 48.2 (1997): 363–67.

[x] G. K. Beale, "Positive Answer to the Question: Did Jesus and His Followers Preach the Right Doctrine from the Wrong Texts? An Examination of the Presuppositions of Jesus' and the Apostles' Exegetical Method," in *The Right Doctrine from the Wrong Texts?* ed. G. K. Beale (Grand Rapids: Baker, 1994), 394, 398; similarly: Dodd, *According to the Scriptures*, 130.

[xi] See: Colin Hamer, *Marital Imagery in the Bible: An Exploration of Genesis 2:24 and its Significance for the Understanding of New Testament Divorce and Remarriage Teaching* (London: Apostolos, 2015), §1.2

[xii] When in John 8 Jesus says that the father of the unbelieving Jews is not Abraham, but the devil, he does not mean the latter literally. Rather, it is that just as Abraham is the 'head' of the Jewish nation, so the devil, as the husband, is the 'head' (Ephesians 5:23) of unbelieving humanity exiled from Eden.

[xiii] Dr Richard Congdon lists twenty-one reasons why Jesus came: http://www.teachinghome.com/em-elements/christmas/21reasons.cfm

[xiv] Lyrics © Warner/Chappell Music, Inc., The Lorenz Corporation; Lyrics Licensed & Provided by LyricFind.

www.ingramcontent.com/pod-product-compliance
Lightning Source LLC
LaVergne TN
LVHW020100090426
835510LV00040B/2667